Vegilovers' Delight

A Cook Book

Kusum Lata Agarwal

bfa

Books For All

(an imprint of Low Price Publications)

Delhi-110052

Distributed by
D.K. Publishers Distributors (P) Ltd.
4834/24, Ansari Road, Darya Ganj,
New Delhi-110 002
Phones : 23278584, 23278368, 23261465
e-mail : dkpd@del3.vsnl.net.in
Visit us at : www.dkpd.com

First published 2004

Published by
Book For All
(An imprint of Low Price Publications)
A-6, Nimri Commercial Centre,
Near Ashok Vihar Phase-IV,
Delhi-110052
Phones : 27401672,27452453
e-mail : lpp@nde.vsnl.net.in
visit us at : www.lppindia.com

Designed at
D K Expressions, Delhi Ph.: 27104684

Printed at
D K Fine Art Press P Ltd.
Delhi-110052

For more Recipes
Please log on to the Author's website at : www.vegilovers.com

PRINTED IN INDIA

PREFACE

I was born and brought up in a traditional Indian vegetarian family. Being the only daughter, I used to help my mother in preparing vegetarian dishes. Soon, I started to enjoy cooking and regularly experimented with different dishes; which led to developing many new recipes.

Afterwards, I got married in a Marwari family, and learnt a lot of Rajasthani dishes from my mother-in-law. Having lived in Thailand, the Philippines and Egypt, I used to make a variety of dishes using local ingredients, which our guests used to enjoy even more then non-vegetarian food. They were surprised to see that so many delicacies could be made in vegetarian food, and used to ask for recipes, since the food was tasty as well as, very healthy.

Encouraged by the demand from our guests and friends, I decided to put all my recipes together and launch a website (www.vegilovers.com). The website has been very successful and I have received a positive response.

My son is in the US for his studies. He is also a vegetarian and misses home food. Whenever I visited the States and invited his friends at home, they used to enjoy the vegetarian food very much. Since the students do not have much time to cook, they used to ask for recipes that could be made easily and quickly. My son's friends encouraged me to write a book, which would be handy and a helpful guide for cooking. This tempted me to write **Vegilovers' Delight**

After gathering my favourite and popular recipes, I selected the most delicious and healthy ones for this book. These recipes are designed keeping in mind the ingredients that are easily available around the globe, without sacrificing taste and nutrition.

I hope this book will be useful not only for the vegetarians, but also everyone around the world, who would like to continue enjoying variety of vegetarian dishes to suit their taste and keep themselves healthy.

There is a section on "Handy Tips" and "Home Remedies" to make a complete book for everyday home needs.

This enormous task of launching the website and writing the book would not have been possible without the tremendous efforts put in by Mr. S Ramesh and Mr. Sunil Kumar, who arranged all the recipes and the photographs. I am very grateful to them for their efforts.

Kusum Lata Agarwal

CONTENTS

Drinks...

Nutritious Cocktail

Preparation time : 10 minutes
Servings : 4 glasses

INGREDIENTS

I cup cucumber (grated)
I cup carrot (grated)
I cup lettuce (grated)
I cup spinach (chopped)
2 tsp. coriander leaves
Few leaves of mint
Sugar to taste
Salt & pepper
Crushed ice cubes

METHOD

Extract the juice of all vegetables in a juicer. Adjust salt, pepper & sugar to taste.

SERVING TIPS

Add crushed ice and serve.

Tiranga Fruit Juice

Preparation time : 10 minutes
Servings : 3 glasses

INGREDIENTS

1 cup cantaloupe pieces (green)
½ cup banana pieces
½ cup fresh strawberries
2½ tsp. Sugar
½ cup fresh milk

METHOD

Blend cantalope pieces in blender and keep aside.
Now blend banana pieces with the milk and 1 tsp. sugar and keep aside.
Now blend strawberries with the rest of the sugar and take it out. Keep all the three juices in the freezer to make it chilled. To serve, in one tall glass pour banana juice 1/3 of the glass, then strawberry and on the top cantalope juice.

SERVING TIPS

Serve immediately.
It looks so tempting and delicious too.

Fruity Yoghurt Shake

Preparation time : 6 - 8 minutes
Servings : 2 glasses

INGREDIENTS

1 cup skimmed milk
½ cup strawberries, apricots, peaches and pineapple
½ cup plain yoghurt
6-8 cubes ice
1 tsp. lemon juice

METHOD

Put all the above ingredients in a blender and whip until creamy.

SERVING TIPS

Serve chilled.

Green Mango Panna

Preparation time : 15 minutes
Servings : 8 glasses

INGREDIENTS

2 large hard green mangoes
1 small bunch of mint leaves
1 tsp. black salt
1 tsp. roasted cumin powder
1 tbsp. sugar
1 green chilli (chopped)
2 tbsp. Boondi (small fried savoury from Gram Flour)

METHOD

Boil the mangoes. Let it cool. remove the skin and mash mangoes into pulp. Put mango pulp, mint leaves and green chillies in the mixer and blend it. Add 4 cups of cold water and blend it again. Now strain it. Add salt, sugar, black salt, roasted cumin powder and stir properly. Keep it in the freezer for sometime.

While serving put few boondies in the glass, and fill it with the green Mango panna.

SERVING TIPS

Serve cool.

Shahi Lassi

Preparation time : 20 minutes
Servings : 4 glasses

INGREDIENTS

2 cups fresh yoghurt
3 cups fresh milk
2 tbsp. Sugar
4 tsp. Honey
1 tsp. chirongi (nuts)
1 tsp. pistachios, chopped
½ tsp. cardamom powder
2 pinches saffron (soaked in milk)
1 cup crushed ice

METHOD

Mix milk and sugar together. Boil it, till it becomes thick. Now mix together yoghurt half of thick milk, honey and ice. Beat it with beater. Pour in the glasses (¾ of glass) then pour remaining thick milk on the top of the glasses.

Decorate with pistachios and chirongi.

SERVING TIPS

Serve Chilled.

Appetizers...

Zucchini Soup

Preparation time : 5 minutes
Cooking time : 15 minutes
Servings : 4 persons

INGREDIENTS

6 large zucchinis
2 cups milk
2 tsp. sugar
1 tbsp. butter
¼ cup culiflourets
A pinch of baking soda
Salt and pepper to taste
A few basil leaves, chopped

METHOD

Peel and cut zucchinis in small cubes. Boil cauli florets and 2 tbsp zucchini cubes together. Let it cool. Grind in mixer with a little water. Melt butter in a frying pan and add zuccihini cubes in it. Roast or stir fry for 2-3 minutes on low heat. Then add salt, sugar, soda and a little water and cover it. When zucchini is soft, add milk, grounded cauliflour mixture, black pepper and basil leaves. Simmer for 10 minutes.

SERVING TIPS

Serve hot

Quick Apple Soup

Preparation time : 5 minutes
Cooking time : 15 minutes
Servings : 4 persons

INGREDIENTS

2 apples grated (red and juicy)
2 potatoes, cubed
2 cucumbers cubed
2 tbsp. white pumpkin slices
2 cups milk
Salt and pepper to taste
1 tsp. Sugar
1 tsp. Butter

METHOD

Boil, potatoes, cucumber and pumpkin together with 1 cup water in pressure cooker. When it is cool, blend it in mixer.

Heat butter in a pan, add blended stock to it and add salt, pepper and sugar also. Boil it uncovered. Now add milk and boil it again for 3-4 minutes. Add grated apples to the soup and simmer for 3 - 4 minutes.

SERVING TIPS

Serve hot

Mushroom Potli Soup

Preparation time : 15 minutes
Cooking time : 15 minutes
Servings : 4 persons

INGREDIENTS

4 large Tomatoes
2 Zucchinis
2 Cucumbers
4 tbsp. Mushroom (canned), chopped
Few sheets of Puff Pastry
Salt and Pepper to taste
1 tsp. Sugar
1 tsp. Lemon Juice
A pinch of Ajino-moto
Oil for frying
1 tsp. Butter
2 tbsp. Spring Onions - chopped very fine with leaves

METHOD

Wash and cut tomatoes and zucchinis into cubes. Peel and cut cucumber into long slices. Boil all together with enough water in pressure cooker for 5 minutes. Then remove from heat. Take out cucumber slices. Grind rest of the mixture in a grinder. Strain it and boil it again. Add salt, pepper, sugar and boiled cucumber and boil for few minutes. Remove from fire and keep aside.

HOW TO PREPARE MUSHROOM POTLIS

Take one sheet, cut into half and fill a little chopped mushroom in it, and fold it like a potli with the help of water and deep-fry in hot oil for a minute only. Then take it out on the paper towel. While serving, add mushroom potlis into the soup.

SERVING TIPS

Serve hot
This mushroom potli soup is very delicious and nutritious.

Sour & Spicy Vegetable Soup

Preparation time : 10 minutes
Cooking time : 20 minutes
Servings : 4 - 6 persons

INGREDIENTS

¼ cup Cabbage - Shredded
1 Carrot medium size - Chopped, finely
¼ cup French Beans - Chopped, finely
2 tbsp. Capsicum - Chopped, finely
1 Onion - Chopped finely
A few cloves of Garlic - Pounded
2 tbsp. Sugar
1 ½ tbsp. Olive Oil or any Oil
2 tbsp. Butter
5-6 cups of Water
2 pinches of Ajino - moto
Salt and Black Pepper To taste

For Sauce Mixture

2 tbsp. Soya Sauce
1 ½ tbsp. Vinegar
2 tbsp. Corn Flour
1 tbsp. Chilli Sauce
1 cup Water

METHOD

Heat oil, add garlicand stir it a little, then add all vegetables and ajino-moto and cook for 3-4 minutes. Take out 3-4 tbsp. of vegetables and keep aside. Now add water. When mixture starts boiling, cover the pan and cook for 15 minutes on slow heat. Remove from heat and sieve it from fine mash. Boil the soup again. Now mix together all ingredients for sauce and mix into the soup and stir. Add salt, pepper and remaining vegetables to it and stir again for few minutes and remove from heat.

While serving, put 1 tbsp. Butter

SERVING TIPS

Serve hot

Salad...

Mango Moong Salad

Preparation time : 25 minutes
Servings : One large plate

INGREDIENTS

1 cup sprouted green gram (moong)
1 ripe alphonso mango (cut into tiny bites)
4 large potatoes (boiled and mashed)
2 tbsp. Milk
8 cabbage leaves (blanched)
8 cottage cheese pieces (paneer) (cut into petal shape)
2 beetroot (boiled and grated)
1 cucumber (cut into two, length wise)
1 tbsp. lemon juice
Salt & pepper to taste

METHOD

Boil moong in little water for 2 - 3 min. and mix sprouted moong with salt and pepper. Add mango bites and lemon juice and keep aside. Put the mashed potatoes into a piping bag with a nozzle and keep aside. Take a serving dish, shape the moong mango mixture like a mould and place it in the center of dish. Now place cabbage leaves along the sides to make it look like a flower. On each leaf, place paneer pieces as a petal on it. Put some grated beetroot. For a stem, place Cucumber slices and mashed Potatoes all around.

SERVING TIPS

While serving, pick up one cabbage leaf with paneer and beetroot. Add the moong-mango mixture and potato to it and serve.

Sour Wheat Salad

Preparation time : 15 minutes
Servings : 4 persons

INGREDIENTS

1 cup broken wheat, soaked overnight
2 big size tomatoes, diced
¼ cup chopped parsley
2 tsp. chopped mint leaves
2 nos. cucumber, chopped
2 tbsp. chick peas, cooked
Salt and black pepper to taste
¼ cup lemon juice
2 green pepper, chopped
2 tbsp. black olives, chopped
2 tbsp. carrot, grated
1 tsp. crushed garlic
¼ cup olive oil

METHOD

Boil wheat in a pressure cooker with salt for 7-8 minutes. When it is soft, take it out. Now add lemon juice, garlic, olive oil and mint and mix thoroughly, and refrigerate for 2-3 hours. Just before serving, add the vegetables mix gently.

SERVING TIPS

Garnish with olives and serve.

Glass - Noodle Salad

Preparation time : 15 minutes (Excluding soaking time)
Servings : One large plate

INGREDIENTS

3 cups glass noodles (soaked in hot water for one hour)
1 cup green raw papaya (grated)
2 onions (chopped)
2 tomatoes (chopped)
4 green chillis (chopped)
½ cup roasted and crushed peanuts
2 tbsp. Sugar
¼ cup lemon juice
½ cup green gram sprouts (moong)
2 tbsp. fresh coriander (chopped)
Salt to taste
A few slices cucumber, to decorate

METHOD

Mix all ingredients thoroughly. Toss this salad at least one hour before serve so that all the flavors get blend.

SERVING TIPS

Decorate with cucumber slices and serve cold.

Green Raw Papaya Salad

Preparation time : 10 minutes
Servings : 4 - 6 persons

INGREDIENTS

2 cups green raw papaya, grated
1 tomato - chopped
¼ cup roasted and crushed peanuts
¼ cup sprouted moong
Salt & pepper to taste
2 flakes garlic (crushed)
1 onion - chopped
2 nos. green chillis - chopped
1 tsp. Sugar
1 tbsp. lemon juice
1 tbsp. fresh coriander leaves

METHOD

Mix all the ingredients together. Toss this salad for half an hour before serving, so that all the flavors blend.

Chaat...

Raj Kachori Chaat

Preparation Time : 15 minutes
Cooking Time : 20 minutes
Serves : 6 - 8 persons

INGREDIENTS

1 cup Plain Flour
1 tbsp. Semolina
1 tsp. Oil
2 pinches Baking Soda
½ cup Gram Flour (Besan)
1 tsp. Oil
Salt and Red Chilli Powder to taste
A pinch of Asafotida (Heeng)
Oil for frying

METHOD

Mix the flour, semolina, salt, oil and soda, and add enough water to make a firm dough. Cover and keep aside. Mix gram flour, oil, salt, chilli powder and asafotida. Mix very well. Knead the dough again and divide it into equal 15 small portions and roll each portion into small round circles (like poori).

Place ½ tsp. of gram flour mixture in the centre of the circle and fold it and roll it out a little and deep-fry in hot oil over medium flame, till they puff up and are golden brown in colour. While frying, press the kachori, by a flat spoon, till they puff up in the oil. Remove, drain on kitchen paper towel. Repeat the same procedure to prepare all the kachoris.

INGREDIENTS FOR FILLING

1 cup Boiled Green Whole Gram (Moong)
½ cup Boiled Whole Bengal Gram (Kala Channa)
½ cup Boiled Moth
½ cup Boiled Potato Cubes
1 cup Crushed Pakodis
½ cup papdi crushed
1 cup Sev (crisp vermicelli noodles made of gram flour)
1 cup Yoghurt (beated)
½ cup Green Chutney
½ cup Tamarind Chutney
½ cup Chopped Fresh Corriander

METHOD FOR FILLING

Mix all the ingredients except chutneys, yoghurt, corriander leaves and ½ cup sev.

HOW TO SERVE

Prick the kachori in the centre and fill the stuffing and pour 1 tsp. yoghurt and both chutneys on the top. Garnish with corriander leaves and sev. It is very delicious. Serve immediately.

INGREDIENTS FOR PAKODIS

¼ cup Split Black Lentil (Urd Dal)
Salt to taste
¼ tsp. Chilli Powder
A pinch of Asafoteda (Heeng)
Oil for frying

METHOD

Soak lentils for 2 hours in hot water. Drain and grind it coarsely in a grinder using a little water.

Now, add salt, heeng and chilli powder and beat it with a spoon to make it light and fluffy. Drop small portions of the batter into hot oil, and deep fry on slow heat, till the pakodis are golden brown.

Now soak the pakodis in warm water for 20 minutes and then drain and squeeze the pakodis and crush it.

FOR PAPDI

Prepare the same dough like Raj Kachori and roll out very thin round sheet and cut small round or square pieces from it. Deep-fry in hot oil till they are golden.

INGREDIENTS FOR SEV

1 cup Gram Flour
1 tbsp. Oil
Salt to taste

METHOD

Combine gram flour, oil and salt and add water to prepare a smooth dough. Fill this dough into a metal sev maker(machine) and drop sev (vermicelli noodles) in hot oil by pressing the machine. Drain on absorbent paper or towel.

NOTE : Papdi and sev can be made in advance 1or 2 days before.

Potato Basket Chaat

NOTE : These potato baskets are prepared with grated potatoes and with the help of two equal size metal tea strainers.

Preparation Time : 10 minutes
Cooking Time : 20 minutes
Servings : 4 - 6 persons

INGREDIENTS

For the Baskets

2 nos. Big Size Potatoes
2 nos. Tea Strainers (metal)
Oil for frying

For the Filling

I cup Whole Green Gram (boiled)
I cup Moth (brown, boiled)
Black Salt to taste
Salt to taste
Chilli Powder to taste
I tsp. Green Chilli, chopped
I tbsp. Fresh Corriander, chopped
Chaat Masala, to taste
¼ cup Tamarind Chutney
¼ cut Mint Chutney
½ cup Yoghurt (beated)
I cup Fine Sev (made from Gram Flour)

METHOD FOR THE BASKETS

Peel the potatoes and grate thickly in cold water and keep it for 5 minutes. Drain the potatoes and spread over the cloth for 5 minutes. Now divide grated potatoes in equal portions. Place one portion on a strainer and press on the top with another strainer. Hold firmly the strainers and deep-fry in hot oil, over a midium heat till the basket is golden brown. Remove the strainers from the oil and tap softly to unmould the baskets. Repeat the same for other baskets.

METHOD FOR FILLING

Mix all ingredients of the fillings except yoghurt and corriander leaves.

HOW TO PROCEED

Arrange the potato baskets in a serving dish. Now fill I-2 tbsp. of filling in each basket and pour a spoonful of yoghurt on the top. Garnish with chopped corriander leaves and fine sev. Serve immediately.

NOTE : These baskets can be made in advance and Stored in an air-tight box.

Bobby Chaat

Preparation Time : 20 minutes
Cooking Time : 20 minutes
Servings : 6 - 8 persons

INGREDIENTS

I cup Plain Flour
I tsp. Oil
½ tsp. Salt
½ tsp. Baking Powder
A few numbers of biscuit moulds (metal)

For the Filling

I cup Boiled Green Whole Gram(Moong)
I cup Boiled Potato Cubes
½ cup Boiled Chick Peas
I tsp. Black Salt
I tsp. Chaat Masala
Salt and Pepper to taste
½ cup Tamarind Chutney
I tbsp. Onion, finely chopped
I tsp. Green Chilli
I tbsp. Fresh Corriander chopped

METHOD

Mix flour, salt, oil and baking powder and knead a stiff dough, using a little water. Cover the dough with a wet cloth for 10-15 minutes. Rollout the dough into a very thin sheet. Prick all over the sheet with a fork. Then cut round circles from the sheet, using a cooking cutter, and press into biscuit moulds. Heat oil in a frying pan and deep-fry the moulds till they are golden colour. Remove and drain on kitchen paper towel and tap lightly to unmould.

For the Filling

Combine all ingredients for the filling, except chopped corriander, yoghurt and sev. Mix well.

HOW TO SERVE

Fill each bobby mould with a spoonful of filling. Top with yoghurt, Chopped corriander and fine sev. Bobby Chaat is ready.

Serve Immediately.

Semolina Pakodi Chaat

Preparation Time : 10 minutes
Cooking Time : 15 minutes
Serves : 4 persons

INGREDIENTS

1 cup Semolina
2 pinches Baking Powder
Salt to taste
1 tsp. Green Chillies, chopped
1 Onion, chopped
Corriander leaves for garnishing
¼ cup Tamarind Chutney
½ tsp. Ginger Powder
Oil for frying

METHOD

Mix semolia, salt and baking powder, and prepare a thick batter with hot water. Deep-fry little lemon size balls (pakodis) in hot oil.

Boil ½ of tamarind chutney with ginger powder and ½ cup of water. Add hot pakodis in this and boil it again for a few minutes.

Now arrange all pakodis in a serving dish. Spread chopped onion, green chillies and tamarind chutney. Garnish with chopped corriander leaves.

SERVING TIPS

Serve hot

Snacks...

Steamed Zuchini Rolls

Preparation time : 10 minutes
Cooking time : 15 minutes
Servings : 4 persons

INGREDIENTS

4 nos. Zucchini
2 tbsp. wheat flour
1 tbsp. gram flour (besan)
2 tbsp. Semolina
1 tbsp. Yoghurt
2 tbsp. Oil
1 chopped green chilli
1 tsp. crushed coriander seeds
1 tsp. ani seeds. Crushed
1 tsp. carom seeds (ajwain)
A pinch asafoetida (hing)
Salt & pepper to taste
1 tbsp. Chopped coriander leaves
1 tsp. dry mint powder
1 tsp. Lemon juice
1 tsp. Sugar
2 small pcs. dry red chillies

METHOD

Peel and grate zuchinis. Now add all other ingredients (except ajwain, 1 tbsp. of oil and red chillis) together. Bind this mixture very well. Make rolls with oily hands. Now boil water in a big pan and put one strainer on it, to steam and spray little oil on it and arrange all zucchini rolls over this strainer. Cover with the lid for 15 minutes. After 15 minutes, remove the lid and check with a sharp knife. Let it cool. Now cut into small rolls. Now heat 1 tbsp. oil. Put mustard seeds and ajwain. When it crackles, put red chillies and pour this over zuchini rolls. Decorate with coriander leaves.

SERVING TIPS

Serve hot

Spinach and Corn Patties

Preparation time : 10 minutes
Cooking time : 10 minutes
Servings : 3 - 4 persons

INGREDIENTS

2 cups Fresh Spinach
½ cup Corn, boiled
¼ cup Cheese, grated
Few slices of bread
Salt and Black Pepper to taste
Oil for frying

METHOD

Clean, wash and chop the spinach very thin and leave it in the strainer for some time. Now mash the bread slices and mix with the spinach to bind it, like a dough. Then put salt and pepper in it and mix properly. Mix together corn and grated cheese for the filling. Now take some portion of spinach dough on the palm spread it and fill ½ tsp. mixture of corn and cheese. Roll the ball and make pattis shape. Then fry the patties till golden brown.

SERVING TIPS

Serve Hot with Mint Chutney or Tobasco

Baked Potato Pizza

Preparation time : 5 minutes
Cooking time : 20 minutes
Servings : 2 Persons

INGREDIENTS

2 large-sized potatoes
2 big onions (chopped)
2 green chillis (finely chopped)
A small piece ginger (finely chopped)
4 big tomatoes (chopped)
1 tbsp. coriander leaves
1 tsp. red chilli powder
½ tsp. all spices (garam masala)
1 capsicum (chopped)
1 cheese cube
1 tsp. sugar
Oil for frying
Salt to taste
For garnishing : 1 tomato

METHOD

Peel the potatoes and cut into round slices. Fry till potatoes become brown and crispy. Heat 2 tbsp. of oil, add onion, ginger, green chili and fry for 2-3 minutes. Add tomatoes, capsicum and sugar. Sauté for 2 minutes. Add spices, salt, coriander leaves. Mix well. Arrange the slices on a baking tray. Spread the fried masala on the slices with grated cheese. Bake in preheated oven at 250 F (degree) for 7-8 minutes. Garnish pizza with tomato slices.

SERVING TIPS

Serve hot with Tabasco sauce.

Vegetable Potli Samosa

Preparation time : 20 minutes
Cooking time : 15 minutes
Servings :18-20 Samosas

INGREDIENTS

2 cups plain flour
1 tbsp. oil
1 tsp. Salt

Stuffing

2 tbsp. chopped carrots
2 tbsp. boiled green peas
1 tbsp. chopped beans
1 tbsp. chopped bell pepper (optional)
1 tsp. chopped green chilli
1 tbsp. chopped coriander leaves
1 tsp. chopped basil leaves
Salt, pepper to taste
½ tbsp. lemon juice
½ tbsp. sugar
Few pieces raisins and cashew nuts (chopped)
A pinch red colour

METHOD

Make a soft dough from white flour by adding oil and salt, and keep aside. Chop all the vegetables very fine. Now cook in a frying pan in one tsp. of oil for 2-3 minutes. Add salt, pepper, sugar, lemon juice and dry fruits to it and let it cool. Roll small pooris from the dough and fill it with the small portion of the stuffing and make potli shape. Mix red colour to a small portion of the dough. And roll this dough in a very thin chappati and cut strips like ribbon. Now bind the potlis on the top with the strips by wet hand. Fry these potlis till light pink colour.

SERVING TIPS

Serve with green or red chutneys.

Paneeri Golden Balls

Preparation time : 20 minutes
Cooking time : 10 minutes
Servings : 4 persons

INGREDIENTS

4 pcs. medium size potatoes
¼ cup grated cottage cheese (paneer)
2 tbsp. coconut (grated)
1 tbsp. chopped green chillies
1 tbsp. chopped ginger
Cashew nuts - a few pieces
Raisins - a few pieces
Salt and pepper to taste
1 tbsp. Corn flour
1 tbsp. mint chutney
Oil for frying

METHOD

Boil the potatoes and mash very well.

Mix paneer, coconut powder, green chutney, green chillies, dry fruits, salt and pepper all together. Take some portion of mashed potatoes, fill paneer mixture in it and make round ball of it. Make thin corn flour paste with water. Roll this ball in corn flour paste and deep fry in hot oil till it becomes golden color. Take out from the oil. Keep it on paper towel to absorb oil. Cut exactly 2 half pieces and put green and red chutneys on it.

SERVING TIPS

Serve hot

Dhokla

Preparation time : 10 minutes
Cooking time : 20 minutes
Servings : 4 - 6 persons

INGREDIENTS

1 cup Semolina
A few curry leaves
1 cup gram flour (besan)
1 ½ tsp. Fruit Ino Salt
¼ cup Grated Coconut
1 cup Sour Curd
Few coriander leaves
3-4 green chillies
Salt to taste
A small piece of ginger
4 flakes garlic optional
1 tsp. Mustard seeds
3 tbsp. Oil

METHOD

Mix together semolina, gram flour, curd, salt and water ; then leave it to ferment overnight. Add garlic and chillie to the mixture and grind together. Add ino salt to the batter and beat it lightly. Grease a deep plate (thali) with little oil and pour batter in it. Steam it for about 15 minutes. When cool, cut into cubes. Heat oil and add mustard seeds. When it splutters, add curry leaves and pour over dhokla. Garnish with grated coconut and coriander leaves.

Vegetables...

Dal & Kadhis...

Chapathis...

Rice...

One Meal Dish...

Main Course...

Basant Bahar

Preparation time : 20 minutes
Cooking time : 15 minutes
Servings : 4 persons

INGREDIENTS

6 medium size green tomatoes
1 cup gram flour (besan)
2 med. onions (finely chopped)
2 big tomatoes
5 flakes garlic (crushed)
1 tsp. aniseeds
A pinch of asafoetida
¼ tsp. all mixed spices (garam masala)
2 tsp. oil

For Gravy

2 med. onions roasted on flame
2 big tomatoes roasted on flame
½ cup cottage cheese (paneer)
½ tsp. red chilli powder
1 tsp. lemon juice
Salt to taste
1 tbsp. coriander leaves chopped
¼ tsp. turmeric powder
2 tsp. oil
1 tsp. cream
1 tsp. Cumin
Small piece of ginger
2 green chillis
1 tbsp. curd

METHOD

Wash the green tomatoes, and make deep cut in a plus sign, without separating the four parts totally. Heat oil, add asafoetida, onion, garlic, fry for a while. Add besan and fry till golden brown. Put off the fire and let it cool. Add the remaining ingredients, now fill this mixture into the slit tomatoes and keep aside. For gravy, remove skin of roasted onions and tomatoes and then grind onions, tomatoes and ginger, green chillis curd and cream. Heat 1 tsp. oil and add crushed paneer and fry till golden brown. Keep aside. Heat the remaining oil and add asafoetida, jeera and grounded spices paste, and fry it till it leaves the sides of the pan. Add salt, water and stuffed tomatoes. Cover and cook till the tomatoes are done. Sprinkle fried paneer and coriander Leaves.

SERVING TIPS

Serve hot.

Delicious Vegetable Korma

Preparation time : 15 minutes
Cooking time : 20 minutes
Servings : 4-6 persons

INGREDIENTS

1 cup cauliflower florets
2 carrots (cut length size)
¾ cup green peas
1 big piece ginger
2 green chillies, chopped
2 medium sized onions
1 potato
½ cup beans (cut lengthwise)
4 big tomatoes
1 flake garlic
1 bunch coriander leaves
4 tbsp. coconut milk

Spices to be ground

1 piece cinnamon
2 tbsp. coconut
½ teaspoon chilli powder
2 cloves & cardamom (each)
5 pcs. Pepper
½ med sized onion finely chopped

METHOD

Cook all the mentioned above vegetables and keep it separate. Heat oil in a pan and sauté onion; add the ground spice and fry well. Add all the vegetables and cook it for 3-4 minutes until the spices get mixed with the vegetables. Pour the coconut milk and sprinkle the coriander leaves.

SERVING TIPS

Serve hot with bread.

Marwadi Special Aloo

Preparation time : 10 minutes
Cooking time : 10 minutes
Servings : 6 persons

INGREDIENTS

6 medium sized potatoes
1 tsp. coriander seeds
¼ tsp. asafoetida
2 each cloves & green cardamom
1 tsp. cumin seeds
2 nos. whole red chillis
Salt to taste
1 tsp. coriander seeds
1 tsp. dry mango powder (amchoor)
1 tsp. onion seeds
1 tsp. sesame seeds
2 nos. bay leaves
A small piece of cinnamon (dalchini)
1 tsp. Turmeric powder
1½ tsp. crushed peanuts
1 tbsp. ghee or oil
½ tsp. chopped coriander leaves
½ tsp. all spices (garammasala)

METHOD

Wash the potatoes very well. Now cut into round thick slices. Heat the ghee in a fry pan. Put cumin seeds, onion seeds, Asafoetida, bay leaves, cloves, whole red chillis, cinnamon and cardamom. Fry it for ½ minute. Now put potatoes, coriander seeds, peanuts and all the spices except sugar, mustard, powdered sesame seeds and coriander leaves. When potatoes are soft, add sugar, mustard powder, garam masala and sesame seeds and sprinkle coriander leaves also. Cover and keep for 5 minutes on the slow fire. Delicious marwadi style potatoes are ready.

SERVING TIPS

Serve hot with chappati or purees.

Baked Creamy Spinach

Preparation time : 15 minutes
Cooking time : 20 minutes
Servings : 4 persons

INGREDIENTS

I bunch spinach (chopped)
I piece ginger (grated)
½ cup baby corn (lengthwise cut)
4 tomatoes (medium size)
½ tsp. turmeric powder
I tsp. coriander powder
Salt to taste
A pinch of soda bicarbonate
3 green chillis (chopped)
I small onion
I/3 cup cream or malai
¼ tsp. all spices (garam masala)
½ tsp. red chilli powder
½ tsp. dried mango powder (amchur)
3 tbsp. ghee

METHOD

Wash and drain spinach. Boil together with I cup water, spinach, turmeric powder, onion, ginger, chillis and a pinch of soda. When spinach is soft, mash mixture, with a fork or ladle. Cut baby corn lengthwise. Heat 2 tbsp. ghee, add baby corn, cook for 2-3 minutes, then add spinach mixture, salt, amchur, garam masala. Stir and cook till thick. Now add beaten malai or cream. Stir till smooth. Make thick puree of tomatoes. Now heat remaining ghee, add tomato puree, salt, chilli powder and stir for 2-3 minutes. Tomato gravy is ready. Now put half of the gravy in a buttered baking dish, and spread the layer of half spinach over it and again pour tomato gravy over it and another layer of spinach. Now sprinkle 2-3 cubes of grated cheese over spinach and bake for I0 minutes on minimum heat.

SERVING TIPS

Serve hot.

Methi Dumplings

Preparation time : 10 minutes
Cooking time : 15 minutes
Servings : 4 persons

INGREDIENTS

For Dumplings

2 bunches fenugreek (methi) leaves (finely chopped)
¾ cup gram flour (besan)
Salt to taste
I tsp. coriander seeds (crushed)
I tbsp. fresh coconut (grated)
I tbsp. oil for frying
I pinch asafoetida

For Gravy

I tsp. red chilli power
I tbsp. fresh curd (beaten)
I tsp. cumin seeds
½ tsp. turmeric powder
I tsp. green chillis (paste)

METHOD

Mix all ingredients, except yoghurt, Itbsp. Oil, cumin seeds and asafoetida. Form into small oval dumplings. Heat the oil and deep fry these dumplings and keep aside. Now heat I tbsp. oil and add cumin seeds and asafoetida, when it splutters, add beated yoghurt and other spices with little water and stir continuously. When it is cooked, add methi dumplings and keep cover for 2-3 minutes in gravy on the gas.

SERVING TIPS

After that sprinkle coriander leaves and serve hot.

Govind Gatta Rajasthani

Preparation time : 15 minutes
Cooking time : 20 minutes
Servings : 4 persons

INGREDIENTS

For the Gattas

2 cups yellow gram flour (besan)
1 tbsp. turmeric powder
2 tbsp. cottage cheese
1 tsp. chopped coriander leaves
2 tsp. chopped cashew nuts
A pinch of baking soda
1 tbsp. oil
Salt to taste
1 tsp. chopped green chillis
8-10 nos. raisins
1 tsp. coriander seeds

For the Gravy

2 nos. medium size tomatoes
1 tsp. chopped green chillis
2-3 nos. cardamom
1 tsp. mustard seeds
1 tsp. sugar
1 tsp. chopped coriander leaves
1 tsp. turmeric powder
1 tsp. red chilli powder
½ cup fresh cream or malai
1 small piece ginger
6 nos. cashew nuts
1 tsp. cumin seeds
2 nos. bay leaves
2 tbsp. curd
Salt To taste
1½ tsp. coriander powder
1 tsp. Oil

METHOD

For Gattas

Mix besan, salt, oil, turmeric powder and baking soda together. Bind a soft dough by adding warm water. Now mix together cheese, green chillis, salt, raisines, cashews, coriander seeds and leaves. Make small diamond size balls from this stuffing. Take a small portion from the dough and flatten it on the palm, fill stuffing ball in it. Roll this properly in your palm. Make all gatta rolls like this. Heat the oil in a fry pan. Deep fry gattas in the oil and take it out on the paper towel, keep aside.

For the Gravy

Make a fine paste from cashews, ginger chillis and tomatoes. Heat the oil and put mustard seeds, cumin seeds, bay leaves and cloves etc. Let it splutter. Add this paste and fry for 2 minutes. Now add the spices and beated curd and fry continuously till it leaves the sides of the pan. Add some water and gattas stir properly. Sprinkle coriander leaves and Cream on the top.

SERVING TIPS

Serve very hot.

Paneer Pasanda

Preparation time : 10 minutes
Cooking time : 15 minutes
Servings : 4 persons

INGREDIENTS

1 cup cottage cheese (paneer)
2 grated tomatoes
1 tsp. ginger grated
1 tsp. coriander leaves chopped
½ tsp. turmeric powder
½ tsp. all spices (garam masala)
1 tsp. anardana powder (optional)
½ tsp. mustard seeds
1 chopped onion
½ green chillis chopped
½ tsp. garlic crushed
1 tsp. red chilli powder
½ tsp. coriander powder
½ tsp. sugar
Salt to taste
2 tbsp. oil

METHOD

Cut paneer into long strips, keep aside. Now heat oil in a saucepan. Add mustard seeds, when it crackles, add green chillis, ginger and garlic, stir it for 1 minute. Now add grated tomatoes (tomato puree) and cook it for 2-3 minutes or till oil leaves the sides of the pan. Now mix all ingredients with the water properly and add in the tomato gravy. Stir it. Now add paneer pieces in this gravy and cook for 2-3 minutes. Gravy should be thick.

SERVING TIPS

Sprinkle coriander leaves and serve hot.

Green Leafy Vegetable (Hariyali Sabji)

Preparation time : 10 minutes
Cooking time : 15 minutes
Servings : 6 persons

INGREDIENTS

2 small bunches of spinach
1 small bunch of radish leaves
Few leaves of spring onions
A small piece of ginger (chopped)
½ tsp. turmeric powder
½ cup plain beated curd
1 tsp. cumin seeds
1 small bunch dill
1 big bunch mustard leaves
2-3 green chillis (chopped)
½ tsp. grated garlic (grated)
½ tsp. All spices (garam masala)
Salt to taste
A pinch of soda bicarbonate

METHOD

Chop all greens, boil till tender (pressure cook or in plenty of water) with a pinch of soda. Drain and keep aside. Now heat oil in a saucepan, add cumin seeds, when it splutters, add ginger and garlic and stir for a minute. Add chillis, stir. Add turmeric powder and salt, add curds and stir continuously till whiteness is gone completely. Add greens and cook till gravy is almost semi solid. Sprinkle garam masala, stir and remove from heat.

SERVING TIPS

Serve hot with bread, kulcha, etc

Coconut Malai Koftas

Preparation time : 10 minutes
Cooking time : 10 minutes
Servings : 4 persons

INGREDIENTS

I cup coconut powder
2 cube cheese
I tsp. chopped green chilli
2 tbsp. chopped tomatoes
I cup cream
Few chopped coriander leaves
3-4 pcs. Boiled potatoes
I cup bread crumb
2 tbsp. chopped onions
A small piece of ginger
I tsp. salt
Oil to fry

METHOD

Mix coconut powder, potatoes, breadcrumb, salt, coriander leaves, green chillis and cheese together. Bind them in form of small balls, then fry them and keep aside. Make paste of tomatoes, onions and ginger. Fry this paste in little oil. Now put salt, turmeric powder, red chilli powder and stir them. Add a little water and make the curry, after 5 minutes, Put the koftas into the curry.

SERVING TIPS

Serve with cream on top.

Royal Dal

Preparation time : 10 minutes
Cooking time : 15 minutes
Servings : 4 persons

INGREDIENTS

1 cup arhar dal
2 cups milk
1 cup cream
1½ cup yoghurt (beaten)
1 tsp. saffron (soaked in milk)
2 tsp. cumin seeds
1 tsp. mustard seeds
2 nos. chopped green chillis
6 nos. green cardamom
Few chopped mint leaves
4 nos. cloves
Salt & pepper to taste
½ tsp. red chilli powder

METHOD

Boil dal in 3 cups of water till it is tender. Drain excess water. Add milk, cream, curd, cloves, cardamoms, saffron, salt and red chilli powder to dal. Cover and cook for 5 minutes or till the dal gets mixed well. In a fry pan, heat ghee, fry cumin & mustard seeds and asafoetida. Pour dal over it.

Garnish with green chillis and mint leaves.

SERVING TIPS

Serve hot.

Mixed Kathod

Preparation time : 10 minutes (Excluding soaking time)
Cooking time : 25 minutes
Servings : 4 - 6 persons

INGREDIENTS

¼ cup whole green gram (moong)
¼ cup whole lentil (masoor)
2 tbsp. soyabean
¼ cup black eyed beans (lobiya)
¼ cup whole black gram (black urd)

For the gravy

2 medium sized onions
2 flakes garlic
4 medium sized tomatoes
2-3 nos. chopped green chillis
Small piece ginger
½ cup fresh cream
1 tbsp. yoghurt
1 tbsp. ghee
1 tsp. lemon juice
2-3 nos. cloves
Small piece cinnamon
2-3 nos. cardamom
2 nos. bay leaves
2 nos. dried whole red chillies
½ tsp. red chilli powder
½ tsp. turmeric powder
Salt to taste
1 tsp. chopped fresh coriander leaves
A pinch asafoetida
1 tsp. cumin seed

METHOD

Wash all the kathods and soak overnight. Boil in pressure cooker with salt and turmeric powder. After 2 whistles, cook it over slow fire for 10 minutes.

For Gravy

Peel and grate the onion and tomatoes. Chop green chillis, ginger and garlic. Heat ghee in a frying pan, put cumin seeds. When it splutters, add bay leaves, cloves, cinnamon and cardamom and fry it for ½ minute. Now add grated onion and garlic, fry till it becomes light brown color, then add grated tomatoes. Fry again till ghee leaves sides of the pan. Now put red chilli powder, salt, lemon juice and fry it for ½ minute. Now add boiled kathod and mix very well.

Beat the fresh cream and yoghurt together very well and mix in dal (kathod). Close the lid and take one more whistle (boil) in pressure cooker. While serving, heat one tsp. ghee in the sauce pan, put asafoetida, whole red chillis and 2 pinches red chilli powder. When it is very hot, pour on top of the dal. Sprinkle coriander leaves.

SERVING TIPS

Serve very hot.

Mango Kadhi

Preparation time : 10 minutes
Cooking time : 20 minutes
Servings : 4 persons

INGREDIENTS

2 cups curd
½ cup gram flour (besan)
½ cup chopped mango pieces
1 tsp. sugar
1 cup mango pulp

For the seasoning

2 nos. cloves
1 tsp. cumin seeds
1 tsp. mustard seeds
½ tsp. fenugreek seeds
A pinch of asafoetida
1 tsp. chopped green chillis
3-4 nos. curry leaves
½ tsp. turmeric powder
½ tbsp. Ghee

METHOD

Mix curd and besan together, beat very well and add salt and turmeric powder. Heat ghee, add all ingredients for the seasoning and fry for ½ minute. Then add curd and besan mixture, stir constantly till it boils. Now add mango pulp and boil it again for 5 minutes. Add sugar also in it. Add mango pieces and stir it. Cook this kadhi on slow heat for 10-15 minutes. If it is thick, add a little water and cook again for 2 minutes. Now remove from heat. It will give a very good flavor.

SERVING TIPS

Serve hot.

Kabuli Kadhi

Cooking time : 30 minutes
Servings : 4 - 6 persons

INGREDIENTS

2 cups yoghurt
3 tbsp. gram flour (besan)
I cup green fenugreek leaves (chopped)
½ cup moong dal badi
½ tsp mustard seeds
½ tsp. fenugreek seeds
½ tsp. cumin seeds
A pinch of asafoetida
½-½ tsp. turmeric and coriander powder
I tsp. ginger, grated
I tbsp. coriander leaves, chopped
2 Nos. green chillis, chopped
½ tsp. red chilli powder
2 tbsp. oil
2 tbsp. ghee (butter)
Salt to taste

METHOD

Mix yoghurt, besan and water together and prepare a think batter, keep aside. In a frying pan, heat I tsp. oil and shallow fry the badis on low flame, till pink colour. When it is done, take it out from the pan and keep aside. In the same frying pan, heat another tsp oil and put cumin, mustard and fenugreek seeds and let it splutter. Then add asafoetida, ginger, green chillis, roasted badis and I cup water. Cover it and cook it till badis get soft. When it is done, add yoghurt, besan batter and all other ingredients. Let it boil, then simmer on low flame for 15 minutes. When it is little thick, remove from the heat. Temper with hot ghee and red chilli powder.
Garnish with chopped coriander.

SERVING TIPS

Serve with rice or chapatti.

Tikdiya Roti

Preparation time : 10 minutes
Cooking time : 15 minutes
Servings : 6 Rotis

INGREDIENTS

½ cup wheat flour
1/2 cup gram flour (besan)
1 tsp. salt
½ tsp. turmeric powder
½ tsp. chilli paste
A few coriander leaves chopped
¼ tsp. red chilli powder
2 tbsp. ghee or butter

METHOD

Mix together all ingredients except 1 tbsp. Ghee. Knead soft pliable dough with warm water. Cover this dough for half an hour. Knead it again, and divide into small lemon size balls. Take a small ball of the dough and press on a floured board and roll out a thick round and small size tikidi (3"diam). Put this tikidi on a hot tava (griddle), cook for a minute or two and turn once, till golden spots appear. Now cook on low flame directly from both sides. Pinch in the center of the tikdi and put ghee very well.

SERVING TIPS

Serve hot with dal or pickles.

Nutritious Paratha (Sprouts)

Preparation time : 20 minutes
Cooking time : 15 minutes
Servings : 10 Parathas

INGREDIENTS

2 cups wheat flour
1 cup green whole gram (moong sprouts)
1 no. chopped green chilli
1 no. chopped onion
Salt to taste
½ tsp carom seeds (ajwain)
A big pinch asafoetida
2 tbsp. oil

METHOD

Add salt to the flour and make a soft smooth dough by adding warm water. Keep the dough covered with a moist cloth for half an hour. Now crush the moong a little. Heat 1 tsp. Oil in a frying pan and put asafoetida, ajwain and cumin seeds, allow to splutter. Add crushed moong and fry till it becomes dry. Now add onion and green chilli and fry for 2-3 minutes. Add coriander leaves and remove from fire. Let it cool. Knead the dough again very well and take a small portion of the dough, flatten a little, and put a tbsp. of sprout mixture. Cover the mixture by drawing up the edges towards the center, press on a floured board and roll out into a round as large as a saucer. Put the paratha on a hot non-stick griddle, cook for a minute and turn once. After a minute, add a little oil or ghee around the edges. Turn again and cook from other side. When golden patches appear on both sides, the paratha is ready. Repeat for the rest of the dough.

SERVING TIPS

Serve hot with curd or chutneys.

Stuffed-Squash Naan

Preparation time : 30 minutes
Cooking time : 25 minutes
Servings : 15 Naan

INGREDIENTS

For Naan

1 cups plain flour (maida)
1 tsp. yeast
½ tsp. salt
2 tbsp. curd
1 tsp. sugar
2 tsp. oil
1 tsp. onion seeds (kalonji)

For Filling

1 cup grated squash
2 nos. chopped green chillies
1 nos. chopped onion
½ tsp. all spices (garam masala)
½ cup butter
½ tbsp. chopped coriander leaves
Salt to taste

METHOD

For the Naan

Soak sugar yeast and salt together in ½ cup of lukewarm water for 10 minutes. When bubbles come up mix it to flour. Add curd and kalonji also to it and knead into a soft dough. Put a little oil on it and keep covered in warm place for 45 minutes. Knead again very well and keep it covered for sometime again. When it puffs up double, make balls from it by using oil and keep aside.

For the Filling

Put a big spoon of oil in a frying pan. Add cumin seeds when it crackles, put green chillies and onion, fry for two minutes. Now squeeze grated squash and put it into the frying pan. Cook till it becomes dry. Add the spices and coriander leaves also to it. Remove from the heat, let it cool.

How to Proceed

Take one ball and flatten it with a rolling pin with the help of dry flour. Put a spoonful of stuffing in it, and cover it properly, and roll out on the floured surface into triangle shape. Bake in preheated oven till it is golden and crispy. Remove from the oven, put butter on it.

SERVING TIPS

Serve hot with any delicious vegetable.

Pineapple Kulcha

Preparation time : 10 minutes
Cooking time : 15 minutes
Servings : 8 Kulchas

INGREDIENTS

1 cup wheat flour
1 tsp. salt
2 tbsp. plain flour
2 tbsp. oil
½ cup pineapple pieces (crushed)
Salt to taste
½ tsp black pepper
½ tsp. cumin seeds

METHOD

Sift the flours, mix salt and 1 tbsp. Oil. Knead soft dough, cover and keep aside. Mix together pineapple, salt, black pepper and cumin seeds. Now knead the dough again very well. Take a small portion of the dough, flatten a little and put ½ tsp. of pineapple filling in the center, cover the filling by drawing up the edges towards the center. Press on a floured board and roll out into a thick round size poori. Put the kulcha on a hot tava (or skillet) and cook for a minute or two, then turn once after a minute, remove from the tava and cook in a preheated oven till golden patches appear on both of the sides. Press a little in the center of kulcha and put ghee very well.

SERVING TIPS

Serve hot.

Sweet & Sour Pulao

Cooking time : 20 minutes
Servings : 3 persons

INGREDIENTS

1 cup rice
100 gms. plums
¼ cup sugar
1 tbsp. Oil
1 small piece of cinnamon
2 nos. black cardamom
4 nos. cloves
2 nos. bay leaves
2 pinches garam masala
2 cups water
Salt to taste

METHOD

Wash and soak rice in water for 20 minutes. Wash and cut plums into 4 pieces and boil it. Now add sugar, salt and garam masala and cook it for 3-4 minutes, until it becomes little thick, like chutney. Heat oil in a pan, put cloves, cinnamon, cardamom and bay leaves and stir-fry. Add water, salt and rice and cover it. Cook on low flame till it is done. Now in a round bowl, spread the rice, then pour the plum chutney over it and again make layers of rice and chutney. While serving, turn the bowl upside down in a dish and put a few pieces of chopped plums and chutney over it. Sweet and sour pulao is ready.

SERVING TIPS

Serve hot.

Shahi Colourful Rice

Cooking time : 20 minutes
Servings : 4 - 6 persons

INGREDIENTS

2 cups long grain rice
½ cup magaj seeds (cantaloupe seeds)
¼ cup almonds (chopped)
¼ cup makhana (lotus seeds)
2 tbsp. butter
1 tbsp. raisins
1½ tbsp. cashew nut (chopped)
1 cup boiled green peas
1 tbsp. chopped capsicum
¼ cup grated cottage cheese (paneer)
1 onion (cut lengthwise)
1 peeled and chopped tomato
2 tbsp. ghee
Salt to taste
1 tsp. sugar

For Decoration

2 potatoes (medium size)
A pinch of each red, green and yellow color

METHOD

Wash and soak rice for 10-15 minutes Now boil rice in 3½ cups of water, when it starts boiling, add grated paneer and butter and cover it loosely and cook on medium heat. When it is cooked, put off gas. Now heat ghee in a frying pan, put makhana, almonds, cashew nuts, raisins, magaj seeds and fry it little and remove from the frying pan. Keep aside. In the same remaining ghee, fry onions and chopped capsicum for 3-4 minutes. Add chopped tomatoes, boiled peas, salt and sugar to it. Now mix all together, rice, dry fruits and vegetables very well.

For Decoration

Peel and grate potatoes very fine in water. Squeeze out water and divide into three portions. Now mix a pinch of red, green and yellow colour to all three portions of potatoes. Heat oil in a frying pan, fry these colored grated potatoes and drain, one by one. Now in a serving dish, put rice and spread these colorful potatoes on the top.

SERVING TIPS

Serve hot.

Baked Coriander Rice

Preparation time : A few minutes
Cooking time : 30 minutes
Servings : 4 persons

INGREDIENTS

1½ cup long grain rice
½ cup chopped coriander leaves
1 sliced tomato
1 sliced onion
2 tsp. garlic - ginger paste
1 tbsp. oil
¼ tsp. black pepper
Salt to taste
2 tbsp. grated cottage cheese

METHOD

Wash and soak rice for 10 minutes, then boil it and keep aside. Heat ½ tbsp. oil in a frying pan, put ginger-garlic paste, fry it. Then add chopped coriander, salt and black pepper, and cook it for a while. Now heat other ½ tbsp. of oil, put onion and tomato, stir-fry for 2 minutes. Now add rice and salt into it. Mix well. Now put half of rice, in a baking dish, then half of coriander layer and then again other half rice and on the top, coriander. On the top, decorate with onion and tomato slices. Spread grated cheese over it and bake it for 20-25 minutes at medium heat in oven.

SERVING TIPS

Serve hot.

Kesri Pulao

Preparation time : A few minutes
Cooking time : 20 minutes
Servings : 4 persons

INGREDIENTS

Sweet

2 cups long grain rice (basmati)
2 pinches saffron (soaked in milk)
A pinch of yellow colour
1 tbsp. sugar
2 nos. green cardamom
1" cinnamon
2 bay leaves
2 cloves
1 tbsp. chopped almonds and cashews
1 tsp. raisins
½ tbsp. Ghee

Namkeen (salted)

1 boiled potato (medium size)
¼ cup boiled peas
1 tsp. Green chopped chilli
1 tsp. mustard seeds
1 tsp. coriander seeds
1 tbsp. chopped fresh coriander leaves
2-3 sweet neem leaves
½ tsp. dry mango powder
Salt to taste
½ tsp. red chilli powder
2 cloves
1 tsp. chopped cashew nuts
1 tbsp. Oil

METHOD

Wash and soak rice for 15 minutes. Now boil rice with a pinch of saffron and color. Divide the rice into two parts.

For Sweet

Heat ghee in a vessel. Put cloves, bay leaves and cinnamon and fry it. Now add cardamoms, raisins, cashew nuts and almonds, fry it. Then add boiled rice (1/2) to it and mix well. Put sugar and soaked and mashed saffron also and again mix very well, cover it and cook it on low heat for 3-4 minutes. Then Keep aside.

For Namkeen

Heat oil in a frying pan. Put mustard seeds, when it splutters, add coriander seeds, sweet neem leaves, cloves and cashew nuts, let it fry for ½ minute. Mix together, boiled rice(1/2), salt, red chilli powder, green chillis, dry mango powder, chopped boiled potatoes and green peas. Add rice and masala mixture to the frying pan. Mix well, cover and cook on low heat for 6-7 minutes till everything gets mixed properly. Now put off the gas, remove the cover and sprinkle chopped coriander leaves.

SERVING TIPS

Serve kesri pulao with kadhi or curd.

Nutritious Kichidi

Preparation time : 20 minutes
Cooking time : 20 minutes
Servings : 4 persons

INGREDIENTS

½ cup rice (washed & soaked 30 min)
1 bay leaf
½ cup masoor dal [lentil] (washed & soaked 30 min.)
3 green cardamoms
1 stick cinnamon
½ tbsp. chenna dal [black gram] (washed & soaked 30 min)
½ tsp. cumin seeds
3 cloves
¼ cup shelled peas
½ diced carrot
¼ cup sliced onions
1 tsp. grated garlic
5 baby potatoes clean washed
Salt to taste
1 tsp. grated ginger
4 cups water
3-4 green chillis finely chopped
2 tbsp. ghee
½ tsp. turmeric powder
½ tsp. all spices (garam masala)
1 tbsp. Coriander finely chopped

METHOD

Drain dals and rice and keep aside. Semi crush spices (cardamom, cinnamon, cloves). Heat 1 tbsp. ghee in a large heavy skillet. Add cumin seeds, bay leaf, crushed spices, and let it splutter. Add ginger, garlic, chillis, stir fry for ½ minute. Add onion, potato (with skin), stir-fry for 2 minutes. Add carrots, peas, turmeric, garam masala, salt ; then add dals, rice and gently stir-fry for 1 minute. Add water to it. Heat well and add to skillet. Stir and bring to a boil, cover and simmer till done. Rice and dals should be done but not overdone. Vegetables will get soft and water should be absorbed. Add more water if required in between.

SERVING TIPS

Serve with ghee.

Masala Tikdi In Dal

Preparation time : 20 minutes
Cooking time : 20 minutes
Servings : 3-4 persons

INGREDIENTS

For tikdi

¼ cup wheat flour
¼ cup yellow gram flour (besan)
2 tbsp. corn meal
1 tsp. cumin seeds
1 tsp. crushed whole coriander seeds
1 tsp. ajwain seeds
1 tsp. crushed aniseeds
Salt to taste
1 tsp. turmeric powder
1 tsp. red chilli powder
½ tsp. dry mango powder
¼ tsp. garam masala
1 tbsp. Oil

For dal

½ cup yellow split gram (yellow moong dal)
½ cup archar dal
1 tsp. Turmeric powder
1 tsp. chopped green chillis
1 tsp. grated ginger
1 tsp. mustard seeds
¼ tsp. asafoetida
1 tsp. cumin seeds
1 tbsp. chopped fresh coriander
2-3 nos. whole red chillis
3 nos. cloves
½ cup tomato puree
1 tbsp. Ghee
2 pinches nutmeg powder

METHOD

For Tikdi

Sift all the flours together and mix with all ingredients. Make a hard dough by using warm water. Divide This dough into 10-15 small portions, make round big balls (diamond sized) and press a little with the thumb in tikdi shape. Make all tikdis like this. Boil these tikdis in water for 8-10 minutes. Then remove from the water and keep aside.

For Dal

Wash and soak dals together for 15 minutes. Now boil both of dals in 3cups of water by adding salt, turmeric powder. When dal is cooked, beat it with the hand beater. Now add tomato puree in this. Heat ghee in a small frying pan, put cumin and mustard seeds and let them crackle. Add ginger, green chillis, cloves, whole red chillis, asafoetida and nutmeg powder. Fry a little for ½ minute. Now add dal into it and mix well and put these tikdis and simmer (boil) for 5-6 minutes on the low heat. Cover it.

SERVING TIPS

Sprinkle chopped coriander leaves and serve hot.

Potatoes-Peas Batti (Masala Batti)

Preparation time : 25 minutes
Cooking time : 35 minutes
Servings : 4 - 6 persons

INGREDIENTS

3 cups wheat flour
4 tbsp. ghee
1 tsp. ajwain (carom seeds)
Salt to taste

For filling

2-3 med. size potatoes
1 tsp. green chilli, chopped
1 tsp. crushed whole coriander seeds
½ tsp. dry mango powder
¼ cup boiled green peas
½ tsp. red pepper
1 tsp. crushed aniseeds
Salt to taste
1 tsp. Oil

METHOD

Add ghee to the wheat flour, add salt and ajwain also. Make a semi hard dough with warm water. Cover with a moist cloth and keep aside. Boil the potatoes and mash them very well, add chopped green chillis, salt and other ingredients and fry in a tsp. oil in the frying pan for 5 minutes Let it cool. Now take some portion of the dough on the palm and flatten it. Fill the stuffing and make round ball of it. Repeat for rest of the dough. Boil these balls in water in a large pan. When they float up on the water, put off the gas. Strain these balls. And now bake in pre-heated oven on medium heat till it becomes golden all over. Press a little from the centre of the battis and dip in the hot ghee.

SERVING TIPS

Serve very hot.

Desserts...

Mango Tart

Preparation time : 15 minutes
Cooking time : 30 minutes
Servings : 25-30 pieces

INGREDIENTS

4 med. size ripe mangoes
2 cups pistachios
1/3 cup sugar
(each for almonds/pistachios)
1 tsp. cardamom powder
2 cups almonds
½ cup khoya
(each for almonds/pistachio)
A big pinch Saffron
2-3 nos. Silver sheets

METHOD

Soak, peel and grind Almonds and pistachios in a mixer separately (preferably grate with nut-grater). Mix almonds and sugar together in heavy bottomed frying pan and stir continuously till it starts to leave the sides of the pan. Now add khoya, cardamom powder and crushed saffron in it and stir it very well till it becomes like a soft dough. Keep aside. Repeat the same for pistachios also. Chop mangoes in very thin slices. If mangoes are sour, put a little sugar in it and cook over low flame for 2-3 minutes. When it is dry, remove it. Place a thick layer of pistachio dough smoothly in a serving dish. Spread mango slices over it properly. Now cover it with the almond dough, set properly by hand.

Spread silver sheets over it and keep it in the refrigerator for some time.

SERVING TIPS

Now cut square pieces of the tart and serve it cool. It is very delicious.

Coloured Sandwich

Preparation time : 20 minutes
Cooking time : 40 minutes
Servings : 12 pieces

INGREDIENTS

2 cups chenna
2½ cups sugar
8 cups water
A pinch yellow color
A big pinch saffron

For filling

5 cups milk (for rabdi)
1/3 cup sugar
A pinch saffron (soaked in milk)
1 tsp. cardamom powder
1 tbsp. pistachios (crushed)
Silver foil - few

METHOD

Take half of chenna and mash properly, it should be very smooth, now divide into 5-6 portions. Make flat thick and square shape Sandwich and keep aside. Take another half of Chenna and mix yellow color and crushed saffron in it. Do the same procedure like first one, keep aside. Now boil sugar and water together for 10 minutes. Put white sandwiches in it, boil for 12 minutes and remove from the heat. Let it cool. In the remaining syrup, add a pinch of yellow color and ½ cup of water and boil again. Now boil yellow Sandwiches by same procedure. Let it cool.

For filling

Boil milk and make it thick rabdi, when it remains 1/3 of quantity, put sugar into it and stir very well. Add cardamom powder, saffron and dry fruit mixture to it. Mix well. Let it cool.

How to proceed

Keep white sandwich in a plate. Spread Rabdi over it evenly, now place yellow sandwich to cover it. Press slightly with hand and cut it into triangle shapes. Place in a serving dish according to your choice and spread silver foil over the sandwiches

SERVING TIPS

Serve cool.

Almond Kalash

Cooking time : 30 minutes
Servings :10 pieces

INGREDIENTS

4 med. size ripe mangoes
2 cups pistachios

For Kalash

1 cup almond powder
¼ cup water
½ cup sugar

For the filling

¼ cup pistachio powder
1 tbsp. powdered sugar
1 tsp. ghee
¼ cup crushed cashew nuts & pistachios
½ tsp. cardamom powder

For Decoration

8-10 nos pistachios
Few saffron leaves
8-10 nos almonds
Few silver foil

METHOD

Boil sugar and water; make two threads consistency thick syrup. Now add almond powder to this syrup and remove from the heat. Mix well the mixture, knead very well. Make a dough. Now take small portion of the dough and make a small ball, by using a little ghee in the palms. Fill this ball with the filling and form in a kalash shape. Now decorate the kalash with whole almonds and pistachios. Repeat the same for the rest of the dough. On the neck of kalash, fix a few saffron leaves and pistachio pieces (cut pistachios into thin and long sticks).

Decorate with silver foil all over.

Jaipuri Lahariya

Preparation time : 20 minutes
Cooking time : 20 minutes
Servings : 6 persons

INGREDIENTS

4 med. size ripe mangoes
2 cups almonds
2 cups pistachios
1/3 cup sugar (each for almonds & pistachios)
3 cups fresh milk
1 tsp. cardamom powder
1 tbsp. sugar (for rabdi)
A big pinch of saffron

METHOD

Soak Almonds in warm water for 4-5 hours. Peel and grind almonds. Preferably grate with the nut grater. Now add 1/3 cup of sugar to the almonds and cook on medium heat in a heavy bottomed frying pan. When it forms soft dough, put off the fire. Keep aside. Repeat the same with pistachios. Now boil the milk on low heat till it remains 1/3 of it. Then add sugar, cardamom powder and soaked saffron in the rabdi.

How to Proceed

Now arrange almond dough in a baking dish. Then cover this dough with the pistachios dough, set properly by hand. Now pour the thick Rabdi over it, properly. Bake in a preheated oven, on medium temperature till it becomes light golden color on the top. Then remove from the oven. Let it cool slightly. Then put in the refrigerator. While serving put the silver foil on it.

SERVING TIPS

Serve cool. It is very delicious.

Mal-Pua with Rabdi

Preparation time : 10 minutes
Cooking time : 40 minutes
Servings : 15 pieces

INGREDIENTS

For Mal-pua

2 cups milk
1½ cups plain flour (maida)
A few saffron leaves
Ghee for frying
1 tsp. cardamom powder
A pinch of baking powder

For Sugar Syrup

3 cups sugar
1 cup water
A few saffron leaves soaked in milk

For Rabdi

2 cups milk
1 cup fresh cream (malai)
2 tbsp. sugar
1 tbsp. chopped pistachios

METHOD

For Mal-Pua

Boil the milk, stir continuously till it reduces to half. Let it cool. When it is cool, add maida in it and stir it. Mix it well. Batter should be like pakora batter.

For Sugar Syrup

Mix sugar and water in a big pan. Boil till it becomes sticky in fingers. Now put ghee in a fry pan and put a big spoon full of batter in it, and fry it, and put these fried mal puas in hot chasni (sugar syrup).

For Rabdi

Add malai in the milk and boil it, and make it thick. When it remains half, then add sugar, saffron and cardamom powder in it.

SERVING TIPS

Arrange mal-puas in a plate and put rabdi and chopped pistachios on the top of the mal puas and Serve hot.

Baked Apple Delight

Preparation time : 5 minutes
Cooking time : 20 minutes
Servings : 4 persons

INGREDIENTS

2 nos. red apples
1 cup thick milk (rabdi)
4 nos. sweet and salted biscuits
2 cups water
3 tbsp. mix fruit jam or strawberry jam
½ cup sugar
1 tbsp. chopped cashew nuts & raisins

METHOD

Peel, wash and cut round thick slices of apples. Mix sugar and water together and boil it. Put apple slices in the water and boil it for 10 minutes. When it is just soft, take it out from syrup and arrange in a baking dish. Now fill jam in the centre holes of the apples. And pour a little jam all over in the dish also. Now put rabdi over the apples and spread nuts over the rabdi. Then crush biscuits and spread over it properly. Now bake it for 5-7 minutes, in the oven at medium temperature. When it becomes golden color on the top, take it out. Let it cool slightly and keep it for half an hour in the refrigerator.

SERVING TIPS

Serve cool.

Strawberry Pudding

Cooking time : 20 minutes (excluding freezing time)
Servings : 1 medium dish

INGREDIENTS

2 cups milk
½ cup sugar
1 tbsp. custard powder
(strawberry flavour)
1 thin layer sponge cake
¼ cup water
½ cup chopped fresh strawberry
¼ cup strawberry jams
½ cup fresh cream

METHOD

Pour ¼ cup cold milk to custard powder and stir very well. Boil the milk and put sugar and stir it for 2-3 minutes Now add custard powder to the milk and stir constantly for 4-5 minutes. Keep aside. Let it cool. Spread a thin layer of the cake in serving dish. Mix 2 tsp. sugar into water and sprinkle this syrup over the cake. Now spread strawberry pieces over the cake, and then jam also. Then pour custard layer over it. Again make one layer of strawberry pieces, jam and custard. Now keep the dish in refrigerator for ½ an hour to set the pudding, after that, take it out and spread cream very smoothly on the top.

SERVING TIPS

Serve cold.

Pista Pan

Preparation time : 15 minutes (excluding soaking time)
Cooking time : 35 minutes
Servings : 20 Pans

INGREDIENTS

2 cups pistachios
2 cups sugar
2 tbsp. almonds (chopped)
Few leaves saffron (soaked in milk)
2 tsp. cardamom powder
1 tsp. mava (khoya) (optional)
3-4 nos. silver sheets

METHOD

Soak pistachios in warm water for 15 minutes. Remove Pistachios from water and remove the skin by rubbing it. Now grate Pista by a grating machine (Nut Grater) or grind in mixer. Put sugar and Pista together in a heavy bottomed pan. Roast for 10 minutes, when it leaves the sides of the pan, remove from fire. Let it cool. Now make balls from Pista mixture and roll out small pooris. Then cut from the centre into two pieces and fold in a pan shape. Mix almonds, cardamom powder, saffron and a little sugar and one tsp. Mava (optional) together. Fill pan from the almond stuffing and press properly from the top. Roll in the silver sheet all over.

SERVING TIPS

Decorate in the dish and serve.

Heera Kani

Cooking time : 35 minutes
Servings : 15 Nos

INGREDIENTS

1 ½ cup chenna
1 cup fresh cream
1 tsp. cardamom powder
A few leaves Saffron

For Sugar Syrup

3 cups sugar
6 cups water
A pinch or a few drops of green color

METHOD

Mash Chenna by adding green color gently, make it smooth. Divide the portions and make it flat and oval shapes rasgullah. Boil sugar and water together to make a thin syrup. Add a pinch of the green color to the syrup. Now add all Rasgullahs in the syrup and boil for 12 minutes with lid on high flame. Keep hot water (approx.1kg) in another vessel aside. Now remove all Rasgullahs from the syrup and put in the hot water, and add one-cup sugar syrup also to it. Leave for 2-3 hours. Now mix cardamom powder to the cream and beat well. Remove rasgullas from the water and place on a dish. Cut a small portion from the top of it in an oval shape and fill with the cream and press slightly. Sprinkle saffron leaves on the top. Do the same with other Rasgullahs. Keep it in refrigerator for some time.

SERVING TIPS

Serve cool Delicious and tempting Heera Kanis are ready to eat.

Cashew Tacos

Cooking time : 30 minutes
Servings : 10 pieces

INGREDIENTS

For Tacos

1 cup cashew nut powder
½ cup sugar
¼ cup water
½ tsp. cardamom powder

For Stuffing

½ cup pistachios & almond powder
¼ cup crushed mava
¼ cup powdered sugar
1 tsp. ghee if needed

METHOD

Boil sugar and water together to make a little thick syrup (2 thread consistency) on slow heat. Add cashew nut powder, ghee and cardamom. Stir it well, till it becomes a soft dough. Let it cool. Now divide the dough into small balls. Press the ball and make it in a poori shape and fold it like tacos. Make All the tacos like this. Now mix together pistachio powder, almond powder, sugar, mava and crushed saffron leaves. Fill the stuffing in tacos.

Decorate tacos with silver foil. Place a piece of almond in the centre of the tacos.

Misri Mava

Cooking time : 20 minutes (excluding freezing time)
Servings : 3 - 4 persons

INGREDIENTS

5 cups Milk
1 ¼ cup Sugar
1 ½ cups Cottage Cheese (Paneer)
1 tbsp Cardemom powder
A pinch of Saffron (soaked in milk)
1 tbsp Pistachoes, chopped

METHOD

Boil the milk and stir continuously till it remains half. Then add sugar and stir it for 3-4 minutes. Then remove from the heat and keep aside. Put a little ghee (1/4 tsp) in a non-stick frying pan and add crumbled paneer and ½ tbsp. sugar to it. Roast for a few minutes, till it is dry and then remove from the heat. Now add this roasted paneer to the thick milk. Stir well. Add cardemom powder and soaked, mashed saffron also to it. Place it in the freezer for at least half an hour.

SERVING TIPS

Serve Cool.

Squash Halwa Kosa

Preparation time : 5 minutes
Cooking time : 15 minutes
Servings : 4 persons

INGREDIENTS

4-6 lg. size squash
¼ cup sugar
¾ cup thick milk or mava
1 tbsp. ghee (butter)
1 tsp. cardamom powder
1 tbsp. pistachios, chopped
A pinch of saffron (soaked in milk)

METHOD

Peel and grate squash. Boil it for 5 minutes. Then drain it and roast in ghee for 5 to 7 minutes until it becomes dry. Now add thick milk and stir well. Then add sugar in the last and stir it again very well. Mix cardamom powder, and soaked and mashed saffron into it. Decorate with chopped pistachios on the top.

SERVING TIPS

Serve hot.

Shahi Tukdi

Cooking time : 15 minutes
Servings : 1 Box (500 gm. Approx.)

INGREDIENTS

5 cups milk
1 cup crushed cottage cheese (paneer)
2 tbsp. milk powder
8 tbsp. sugar
½ tsp. saffron (soaked in milk)
1 tsp. cardamom powder

METHOD

Boil the milk and make it half, then add roasted, crushed paneer, add milk powder, sugar and stir continuously for 8-10 minutes. Now put cardamom powder and saffron (soaked in milk) in it. Let it cool. When it is cool, put this in an ice cream box (covered) and keep it in the freezer, for 2-3 hours. Then remove it, cut cubes and serve it.

Kids Favourite...

Rooh Afja Lassi

Preparation time : 15 minutes
Servings : 2 persons

INGREDIENTS

2 cups yoghurt
3 tbsp. honey
2 cups fresh Milk
2 tbsp. sugar
1 tsp. cardamom powder
2 tbsp. Syrup (Rooh Afja)
1 cup crushed ice

METHOD

Mix milk and sugar together. Cook on slow heat until thick. Let it cool. Now mix all the ingredients, yoghurt, honey, crushed ice and half of thick milk (rabid) and cardamom powder. Add into the mixer and blend it a little. Pour into the tall glasses (half) and put the rest of thick milk and Roohafja, on the top.

SERVING TIPS

Serve cold.

Sweet & Sour Lolli Pops

Cooking time : 30 minutes
Servings : 4

INGREDIENTS

2 potatoes (boiled, peeled and mashed)
2 carrots (peeled, boiled and chopped)
½ cup green peas (boiled and mashed)
1 beetroot (boiled, peeled and mashed)
½ cup sweet corn (boiled and mashed)
1 onion chopped
2 tbsp. coriander leaves, chopped
2 tbsp. corn flour
2 cups breadcrumbs
16 pcs. sugarcane (6 cm long)
Oil for frying
Salt to taste
Capsico sauce to taste

METHOD

Heat a little oil in a pan. Add the onions and sauté till they turn golden brown. Add the potatoes, carrots, peas, beetroot, corn, salt, coriander leaves and the capsico. Mix well for all Ingredients to combine and form a thick mass than can be shaped into cutlets. Add a little water to the flour to make a thick batter. Divide the vegetable mixture into 16 rounds or portions. Dip each ball into the batter and then roll it in the breadcrumbs. Fix on to the sugarcane sticks like a lollipop and deep-fry in hot oil, till golden brown.

Nutritional Value of Each Serving

Calories	:	512 kcal
Proteins	:	13.3 g
Fat	:	16.5 g
Minerals	:	1.8 g
Fibre	:	4.2 g
Carbohydrates	:	77.3 g

SERVING TIPS

Serve hot.

Chinni Minni Burger

Preparation time : 10 minutes
Cooking time : 45 minutes
Servings : 4 persons

INGREDIENTS

For the burger patty mixture

3 potatoes, peeled and mashed
1 tbsp. chenna dal, roasted
1 onion, sliced
2 green chillies, chopped
¼ cup groundnuts, roasted
Oil for frying
1 tsp mustard seeds
A pinch of asafoetida
7-8 curry leaves
Salt to taste
¼ tsp. turmeric powder
2 tbsp. flour
1 tomato, sliced
1 cucumber, sliced
1 slice pineapple
4 leaves lettuce
1 cup cornflakes, crushed
1 cup breadcrumbs
4 burger buns, split in half

METHOD

Heat the oil in a pan and add the mustard seeds. Allow them to crackle and Add the green chillies, asafoetida, curry leaves, roasted chenna dal, turmeric powder and groundnuts. Sauté for a couple of minutes. Add the mashed potato and mix well. Season to taste. Remove from heat and set aside to cool. Mix flour with a little water to form a smooth, thick batter. Divide the potato mixture into four portions and shape each into a patty. Dip each patty in a batter and then coat with crushed cornflakes and breadcrumbs. Deep-fry in oil till crisp and golden brown, or cook on non-stick pan until done. Slice each burger bun into half and place a lettuce leaf on the base. Place slices of tomato, cucumber and pineapple on the lettuce. Place the potato patty over it and cover with the other half of the bun. Repeat to make four burgers.

Nutritional value of each serving

Calories	:	388 kcal
Proteins	:	10.4 g
Fat	:	12.6 g
Minerals	:	1.3 g
Fibre	:	1.2 g
Carbohydrates	:	54.6 g

SERVING TIPS

Serve hot.

Apple Tower

Preparation time : 25 minutes
Servings : 4 persons

INGREDIENTS

2 Nos. Apples (medium size)
6 Nos. Chocolate Cake Slices
½ cup Sugar powdered
½ cup Butter (melted)
1 tsp. Cinnamon Powder
1 cup Custard
1 cup Cream (beaten)

METHOD

Peel the apples and cut into round thick slices. Remove the seeds. Mix together sugar powder and cinnamon powder and sprinkle over the apple slices. Now bake these slices in the oven on 150°. Now cut the cake slices also like apple slices. Apply a little butter on it. Then make a tower with the slices. Like first one cake slice, then apple slice on it and repeat with all the slices like this. In a serving dish, put custard down, then place the tower on it and then put a cream ball on the top of the tower.

Kids will love to reach on the tower in the clouds.

Cool Kids (A Soft Drink with A Fruit Kick)

Preparation time : 10 minutes
Servings : 4 glasses

INGREDIENTS

2 apples, sliced
½ cup strawberries, crushed
2 slices canned pineapple
3 cups pineapple juice
2 cups crushed ice

For the decoration

A few sprigs mint
4 cherries

METHOD

Place the crushed ice in four glasses to fill the base. Blend the strawberries, pineapple slices and the pineapple juice to form a thick juice. Pour over the crushed ice. Float a few slices of apple in the juice. Garnish with a sprig of mint and cherry.

Nutritional Value of each serving

Calories	:	140 kcal
Proteins	:	1.2 g
Fat	:	0.4 g
Minerals	:	0.36 g
Fibre	:	0.81 g
Carbohydrates	:	33.9 g

Stir-Fried Nutty Noodles

Cooking time : 20 minutes
Servings : 4

INGREDIENTS

I cup noodles
3 tbsp. tomato sauce
I tbsp. groundnuts, roasted
I tbsp. cashewnuts
I tbsp. raisins
I medium-sized carrot, julienned
2 capsicums, julienned
3 spring onions with leaves, shredded
I tsp. ajinomoto
2 tsp. soya sauce
Salt to taste
½ tsp. white pepper powder
I tsp. sugar
I ½ tbsp oil

METHOD

Boil the noodles, drain and set aside. Heat the oil in a wok. Add the spring onion and the julienned capsicum and carrot, and sauté for a minute. Add the cashewnuts, groundnuts, raisins and sauté well. Add the sugar, salt, ajinomoto and white pepper and mix it. Now put the noodles and the Soya sauce and mix well. Stir-fry for a couple of minutes.

Nutritional Value of Each Serving

Calories	:	351 kcal
Proteins	:	8.9 g
Fat	:	11.7 g
Minerals	:	1.6 g
Fibre	:	2.1 g
Carbohydrates	:	52.6 g

SERVING TIPS

Remove from heat and
Serve hot.

Fruit Bhel

Preparation time : 10 minutes
Servings : 4 persons

INGREDIENTS

1 cup puffed rice
½ cup sev
1 tsp. cumin
A pinch asafoetida
¼ tsp. turmeric powder
½ tsp. black salt
½ tsp. oil
4 tbsp. sprouted moong (beans)
4 tbsp. boiled peanuts
4 tbsp. tomatoes (chopped)
4 tbsp. (each) apples, oranges and pomegranate.
2 tbsp. coriander leaves (chopped)
2 tsp. lemon juice
2 tbsp. chopped strawberries

METHOD

Heat oil in a pan. Put cumin and when it splutters, add asafoetida, turmeric powder and puffed rice and stir it well. Add salt in it and sev also. Let it cool. Now mix all the ingredients and puffed rice mixture together. Toss very well and serve immediately.

SERVING TIPS

Note : Children don't like to eat fruits. This is the best way to eat the fruits.

Low Calories...

Baked Chick Pea Cutlets

Preparation time : 10 minutes
Cooking time : 20 minutes

INGREDIENTS

1 cup chick peas (kabuli channa)
1 tsp. ginger (paste)
1 tsp. garlic (paste)
1 tsp. chilli (paste)
2 tbsp. coriander leaves (chopped)
2 tbsp. bread crumbs
3 tbsp. curd (thick)
¼ tsp. mint (dry)
2 tbsp. cottage cheese (grated)
2 tbsp. processed cheese (grated)
Salt to taste
Black pepper to taste

METHOD

For Stuffing

Mix paneer and processed cheese with salt and set aside. Soak Channa overnight. Pressure cook with water level ½ inch above Channa. Add a pinch of salt. Give one whistle and sim on the flame for 30 mins. Cool and mash it finely with a rolling pin. Add ginger, garlic, chilli paste, coriander, salt, pepper and 2 tbsp. of curd and mix with a light hand.

Divide the mixture into 10 equal balls. Stuff with 1 tsp. of stuffing and fold like a cutlet and place on a greased baking tray. Mix remaining curd with ¼ tsp. of dry mint and spread over the cutlets. Sprinkle bread crumbs. Bake at 160°C for 10-12 mins. or until done.

Navratan Bake

Preparation time : 15 minutes
Cooking time : 25 minutes
Servings : 4 - 6 persons

INGREDIENTS

I cup black gram, soaked (chana dal)
2 tbsp. yellow lentil, soaked (moong dal)
I cup sour curd
2 green chillies
A small piece of ginger
Salt to taste
I tsp. sugar
I tsp. lemon juice
½ cup grated white pumpkin
2 tsp. eno fruit salt
2 tomatoes, pureed

For garnishing

I tsp. mustard seeds
I tsp. sesame seeds
3 tbsp. chopped coriander leaves
3 tbsp. grated fresh coconut

METHOD

Grind chana dal and urad dal to a paste using curd instead of water. Grind green chillies and ginger to a paste and add to the batter along with salt, sugar, limejuice, white pumpkin and coconut. Mix well. Now add eno. Mix and pour half of the mixture into a greased oven proof dish. Spread the tomato puree on top, followed by the remaining batter. Cook on high in a microwave for 8 minutes or in the gas oven on medium temperature for 15 to 20 minutes. Heat oil and season with mustard seeds and sesame seeds. When they splutter, pour over the baked dish. Garnish with coriander leaves and grated coconut.

SERVING TIPS

Serve hot with tomato sauce and mint chutney.

Steamed Traingels

Preparation time : 10 minutes
Cooking time : 20 minutes
Servings : 4 persons

INGREDIENTS

2 cups semolina (sooji)
1 cup yoghurt
1 tsp. oil
1 tsp. mustard seeds
1 tsp. cumin seeds
Salt to taste
1 tbsp. eno
1 cup sliced mushroom
2 capsicums (chopped)
2 tomatoes
½ tsp. red pepper
1 tsp. mint leaves
3 green chillies (chopped)

METHOD

Roast Semolina in a frying pan and cool. Add salt and make a thick batter using curd. Add seasoning of mustard and cumin. Boil 3 glasses of water. Mix eno with sooji batter and transfer to a greased thali layer ½" thick. Sprinkle mushroom mixture over it. Pour the rest of sooji mixture with green chutney mix (mint & chilli). Steam for 15 minutes and take out and cut into 2" tringels.

Broccoli In White Gravy

Preparation time : 10 minutes
Cooking time : 10 minutes
Servings : 2 persons

INGREDIENTS

3 Stalks Broccoli
1 Carrot
2 Pods Garlic
1" piece of Ginger
1 tsp. Roasted Cumin Powder
½ cup Coconut Milk
½ cup Fresh Milk
1 Red Capsicum
1 tbsp. Oil
2 Green Chillies
Salt to taste
½ tsp. all spices (garnished)

METHOD

Cut the broccoli into florets. Cut the carrots into thin round slices. Chop the capsicum also into round slices. Chop the ginger, garlic and green chillies finely. Heat oil in a pan and fry ginger, garlic and green chillies for 2 minutes. Then add all the vegetables, salt and sugar. Sprinkle a little water over the vegetables and cover it and cook over a low flame till vegetables are soft. Then add coconut milk, fresh milk and continue cooking for 2 minutes. Sprinkle roasted cumin powder and all spices.

SERVING TIPS

Serve Hot.

Low Fat Crunchy Pizza

Preparation time : 10 minutes
Cooking time : 20 minutes
Servings : 2 - 3 persons

INGREDIENTS

2 cups plain flour
A pinch of salt
¼ cup lukewarm water
1½ tsp. sugar
2 tbsp. oil
½ tbsp. dry yeast (heaped)
Ketchup to spread on base
1½ cups onion, capsicum and dry mushroom and herbs
½ cup breadcrumbs (to sprinkle)
½ tbsp. cheese spread

METHOD

Mix oil, sugar and yeast in lukewarm water. Stir well to dissolve. Mix and sift flour and salt. Add yeast mixture to flour and make a soft dough. Cover and keep in a warm place for 4 hours. Make big balls and roll like chapattis. Bake in an oven at moderate temperature for about 8-10 minutes. Remove from oven, put ketchup and cheese spread on base. Give a layer of vegetable filling, sprinkle breadcrumbs and bake till the top becomes golden and crisp.

SERVING TIPS

Cut into wedges and serve.

Thailand...
Egyptian...

International Recipes...

Thailand

Som Tum (Thai Traditional Salad)

Preparation time : 10 minutes
Servings : 1 medium size plate

INGREDIENTS

1 med. size raw papaya
2 lg. size tomatoes (chopped)
1 tbsp. peanuts (roasted)
4 red chillies
4 garlic cloves
1 tbsp. lemon juice
1 tbsp. Sugar

METHOD

Shred the papaya and chop the tomatoes. Pound the peanuts, garlic and red chillies in a mixer and make a paste. Add the shredded papaya to the peanut mixture with lemon juice and sugar.
Mix well and serve

Thai Sweet & Sour Vegetable

Preparation time : 10 minutes
Cooking time : 15 minutes
Servings : 1 Bowl

INGREDIENTS

2 small Carrots
1 Capsicum
2 Spring Onions
2 cup Beans
1 cup Cauliflower (cut into flowerets)
5-6 Pineapple slices
1 tbsp. White Flour
1 tbsp. Oil
Salt to taste
A few Curry leaves and Corriander leaves for garnishing

For Sweet & Sour Paste

2 tsp Tomato Ketchup
2 tsp Chilli Sauce
1 tbsp Lemon Juice
2 tbsp Pineapple Juice
1 tsp Tamarind Paste

METHOD

Cut the carrots into long (one-inch) pieces. Chop the capsicums lengthwise. Chop spring onions also lengthwise. Mix all the ingredients for the sweet and sour paste gently, to form a smooth paste. Mix the white flour into 3 tbsp. of water to form a smooth paste. Heat oil in a pan and add all the vegetables. Add salt to taste and cook over a low flame covering the pan till the vegetables are tender. Add sweet and sour paste and white flour paste and mix gently. Cook over a low flame for 2-3 minutes and remove from fire.

For Garnishing

Heat one tsp. oil in a pan and add the curry leaves. Garnish the prepared vegetables with the curry leaves and chopped coriander leaves.

Spicy Rice In Pineapple Boat

Preparation time : 15 minutes
Servings : 4 persons

INGREDIENTS

1 fresh Pineapple
2 cups Cooked Rice
½ cup Coconut Cream
2 Onions
2-3 Green Chillies
2 tbsp Raisins
2 tbsp Cashew Nuts (roasted)
1 ½ tbsp Butter
½ tsp Sugar
Salt to taste

For Yellow Curry Paste

1 tbsp Cumin Seeds (roasted)
1 tbsp Coriander Seeds (roasted)
2 stalks of Lemon Grass (chopped)
2 tbsp Ginger (grated)
½ Onion (sliced)
½ tsp Turmeric Powder
1 tsp Salt
(Grind all the above Ingredients to a fine Paste)

METHOD

Chop the onions and chillies finely. Cut the pineapple lengthwise. Scoop out the flesh with a sharp knife and chop it. Keep another half of the pineapple for using as a dish.

For Yellow Curry Paste

Heat the butter in a frying pan. Add onions and green chillies and fry till it is done. Add the yellow curry paste and fry for another minute. Add the chopped pineapple, cooked rice, coconut cream, raisins and cashews, and stir till it is dry. Add sugar and salt to taste. Fill the rice into the empty pineapple shell. Garnish with coriander leaves and serve hot.

Note : You can use 1 cup of coconut milk in place of coconut Cream.

Thai Green Curry

Preparation time : 10 minutes
Cooking time : 20 minutes
Servings : 1 big bowl

INGREDIENTS

½ cup Baby Corn
2 Spring Onions
1 cup Mushroom
½ cup Long Beans
A few Basil Leaves
2 cups Coconut Milk
1 tsp Sugar
2 tbsp Oil
2 tbsp Thai Green Curry Paste
1 tsp juice of lemon
Salt to taste

For Green Paste

8-10 Green Chillies
2-3 pods Garlic
A few Black Pepper Corns
A small piece of Ginger
1 stalk of Lemon Grass
One small Onion
1 tsp Lemon rind (grated)

METHOD

Cut baby corn and beans lengthwise and keep aside. Cut mushrooms into halves. Cut spring onion also lengthwise. Heat oil in a pan. Add the spring onions, fry a little, then add the mushroom, baby corn and beans and saute for 2-3 minutes. Add the green paste and sugar and continue stirring over a low flame. Add salt to it. Then add coconut milk and mix well. Add basil leaves (keeping aside a few for garnishing) and 1 ½ cup of water. Bring the curry to the boil and continue cooking over a low flame for 5 minutes.

Add the lime juice finely and stir well. Garnish with chopped basil leaves.

Egyptian

Koushari (Egyptian Rice)

Preparation time : 15 minutes
Cooking time : 25 minutes
Servings : 3 persons

INGREDIENTS

- 1 cup brown lentil (ads iswid)
- 3 cups water
- 1 tsp. salt
- 1 cup small macaroni noodles
- 1 cup short grain rice
- 2 tbsp. olive oil
- 1 cup tomato puree
- 2 lg size onions
- ¼ cup olive oil
- 1 or 2 garlic clove (finely chopped)

METHOD

Place lentils in a sieve and wash well under running water. Place in a large pot and add 3 cups water and 1 tsp. salt. Bring to boil, then simmer for 1 hour until tender. Drain and keep aside. Clean same pot and add 4 cups water. Bring to a boil; add 2 tsp. salt and the macaroni. Stir constantly until water returns to the boil and cook, uncovered, for 15 minutes until tender. Stir occasionally. Drain and keep aside. Clean and dry the pot again. Wash rice well in sieve under running water and drain. Heat oil in pot and fry rice over medium heat for 2-3 minutes. Add 2 cups water and 1 tsp. salt and bring to boil, stirring occasionally. Cover and simmer over low heat for 15 minutes or until tender. Leave covered off the heat for 5 minutes for grains to separate. Add tomato puree and bring to the boil. Add lentils and macaroni to cooked rice and toss together lightly with a fork. Pour hot taleya (fried brown onions) and tomato mixture on top, toss again and cover pot. Leave over low heat for 10 minutes.

Taleya

Slice the onion and deep fry in oil till brown colour.

SERVING TIPS

Serve hot.

Hommos Sandwich

Preparation time : 10 minutes
Servings : 4 persons

INGREDIENTS

2 cups boiled chic peas
2 tbsp. roasted sesame
1 tsp. lemon juice
2 nos. green chillies, chopped
½ tsp. black pepper
Salt to taste
1 cup cucumber slices (round and thin)
A few lettuce leaves
4 Egyptian chapattis or nan or pizza base

METHOD

Grind chic peas by adding green chillies, sesame, lemon juice, salt and pepper. Make a smooth paste. Now cut chapattis from the centre and spread the paste. Then place lettuce and cucumber slices.

SERVING TIPS

Serve it cool.

Falafal (with Tahina Sauce)

Preparation time : 10 minutes
Cooking time : 15 minutes
Servings : 4 persons

INGREDIENTS

For Falafal

1 cup fava beans, dried (soaked over night)
½ cup coriander leaves, chopped
1 tbsp. green chillies, chopped
1 tbsp. parsley, chopped
1 tsp. coriander seeds, pounded
2-3 flakes garlic
1 tbsp. lemon juice
Salt to taste
Oil for frying
2 tbsp. sesame

For Tahina Sauce

3 tbsp. sesame
1½ tbsp. split black gram
2 tbsp. yoghurt
1 tsp. lemon juice
1 tsp. olive oil
½ tsp. red chilli Powder
Salt to taste

METHOD

Falafal

Grind the beans coarsely in the mixer. Now add all the ingredients to it and mix very well. Make flat shape balls from it. Apply Sesame seeds on the top and deep fry in oil.

Tahina Sauce

Roast sesame and lentil separately. Then add all other ingredients and grind in the mixer to make it a smooth sauce.

SERVING TIPS

Serve hot with tahina Sauce.

Mahshi

Preparation time : 15 minutes
Cooking time : 30 minutes
Servings : 3 - 4 perons

INGREDIENTS

12 grape wine leaves
1 cup short grain rice
2 large size tomatoes, chopped
1 large onion, chopped
2-3 green chillies, chopped
1 tbsp. coriander leaves, chopped
1 tbsp. parsley, chopped
1 tbsp. basil, chopped
1 tbsp. oil
Salt to taste

METHOD

Blanch the wine leaves and keep aside. Wash the rice and mix all ingredients together. Mix very well. Now clean the leaves and fill rice mixture in it and make rolls by pressing slightly with hand. Then place all the wine rolls in casserole and put 1 tsp oil in it. Put one-cup water in the casserole, and cover the rolls with Aluminium foil and close the lid. Heat it and when water is boiled, simmer on low heat for 20-25 minutes. Then put off the gas. Leave it covered in the steam for some time.

SERVING TIPS

Serve hot.

Note : Potatoes, tomatoes, capsicums and cabbage also can be used in place of grape wine leaves.

STAY FIT

WOMEN - *Height & Weight Chart*

Height	Small Frame	Medium Frame	Large Frame
148 cm (4'10")	44 48 kg	46 51 kg	49 57 kg
150 cm (4'11")	45 49 kg	47 53 kg	51 58 kg
153 cm (5'0")	46 50 kg	49 54 kg	52 59 kg
155 cm (5'1")	48 52 kg	50 55 kg	53 61 kg
158 cm (5'2")	49 53 kg	51 57 kg	55 63 kg
160 cm (5'3")	50 54 kg	53 59 kg	55 63 kg
163 cm (5'4")	52 56 kg	54 61 kg	59 66 kg
165 cm (5'5")	54 58 kg	56 63 kg	60 68 kg
168 cm (5'6")	55 59 kg	58 65 kg	62 70 kg
170 cm (5'7")	57 61 kg	60 67 kg	64 72 kg
173 cm (5'8")	59 63 kg	62 69 kg	66 74 kg
175 cm (5'9")	61 65 kg	63 70 kg	68 76 kg
178 cm (5'10")	63 67 kg	65 72 kg	69 79 kg
180 cm (5'11")	65 69 kg	67 74 kg	70 81 kg
183 cm (6'0")	67 71 kg	69 76 kg	72 83 kg

The wrist is generally considered a good indicator of body frame

Women's Wrist	Under 13.5 cm	13.5 15.5 cm	Over 15.5 cm

MEN - *Height & Weight Chart*

Height	Small Frame	Medium Frame	Large Frame
155 cm (5'1")	51 54 kg	54 59 kg	57 64 kg
158 cm (5'2")	52 56 kg	55 60 kg	59 65 kg
160 cm (5'3")	53 57 kg	56 62 kg	60 67 kg
163 cm (5'4")	55 58 kg	58 63 kg	61 69 kg
165 cm (5'5")	56 60 kg	59 65 kg	63 71 kg
168 cm (5'6")	58 62 kg	61 67 kg	64 73 kg
170 cm (5'7")	60 64 kg	63 69 kg	67 75 kg
173 cm (5'8")	62 66 kg	64 71 kg	68 77 kg
175 cm (5'9")	64 68 kg	66 73 kg	70 79 kg
178 cm (5'10")	65 70 kg	68 75 kg	72 - 81 kg
180 cm (5'11")	67 72 kg	70 77 kg	74 84 kg
183 cm (6'0")	69 74 kg	72 79 kg	76 86 kg
185 cm (6'11")	71 76 kg	74 82 kg	78 88 kg
188 cm (6'2")	73 78 kg	76 84 kg	81 90 kg
190 cm (6'3")	74 79 kg	78 86 kg	83 93 kg
193 cm (6'4")	76 81 kg	80 88 kg	85 95 kg
195 cm (6'5")	78 83 kg	82 90 kg	87 97 kg
198 cm (6'6")	80 85 kg	84 92 kg	89 99 kg

The wrist is generally considered a good indicator of body frame

Men's Wrist	Under 16 cm	16-18 cm	Over 18 cm.

Health Tips

Insect got into Ear

If an insect has accidently got in to your ear, put two drops of honey or castor oil or onion juice to get it out.

Ear Pain

Chop Radish in small pieces and boil in seasame oil till brown color. Then stain the oil and put 2 drops of it in ears.

In garlic juice, mix a pinch of black salt and stir well then put 2 drops of it in the ear for instant relief.

Acidity

Curd is an excellent antacid. Just eat a few spoonfuls when acidity hits you.

Eat one betel leaf (Paan) with four to five peppercorns for three days in the morning.

Stomach Pain

If your child is suffering from Stomatch pain, apply warm asafoetida water on the navel for a quick relief.

Burn

Apply a little tooth paste on burnt skin for immediate relief.

Nutritious Break-fast

Add a couple of mashed ripe bananas to your morning cereal to make it testier and more nutritious.

Constipation

If you suffer from Chronic constipation eat half a cup of blanched spinach.

Take one teaspoon of amla powder mixed with honey daily in the morning

Cold & Fever

For quick relief from cold and mild fever, drink a concoction of ginger juice ajwain (caraway seed) water.

Mouth Freshner

Chewing Cloves not only leaves the breath fresh, but also protects your teeth from germs.

Hair Fall

Add sprouted, dried or powdered fenugreek seeds to coconut oil and massage the scalp. It prevents Hair fall.

Rheumatism

To get relief from rheumatism, massage the affected areas with mustard oil and bathe with hot water.

Indigestion, Acidity, Gas problems

Dry grind and store 100g cummin seeds, 100g aniseeds, 50g caraway (ajwain) seeds and 100g candy sugar. Take half a spoon after regularly after meals.

Hiccups

Chewing a few radish leaves will help to stop an attack of hiccups.

Sinusitis

To get quick relief from Sinusitis, boil half a cup of coconut oil with two teaspoons freshly pounded black pepper corns and apply to the scalp.

Gas trouble

For instant relief from gas, eat one teaspoon of ajwain (caraway seeds)mixed with a pinch of black salt, followed by a glass of lukewarm water.

Swelling wound

To prevent swelling over a wound, apply honey on the affected area immediately.

Health Tips

Kitchen Tips

Bitterness of Bitter gourd

You can remove the bitterness from Bitter gourd by washing it with water in which rice has been soaked.

Food in Tiffin box

During summer, the food carried in tiffin boxes get spoilt. To avoid this, clean and dry the tiffin box and heat it with the lid on till the lid is hot. Pack the lunch in it after the box cools down. This prevents the lunch from getting spoilt.

Nutritious Break-fast

Add a couple of mashed ripe bananas to your morning cereal to make it tastier and more nutritious.

Turmeric Powder

Lightly grease a jar with a little of ghee before putting turmeric powder in it. The turmeric Powder will retain its golden yellow color.

Mashed Potatoes

If you need mashed potatoes in a hurry, peel and cut the potatoes in to small cubes. Boil for 10 minutes and mash.

Chocolate Cake

A pinch of soda bicarbonate darkens the Chocolate cake.

Butter icing

While making butter icing, add a few drops of lemon juice to get the white color.

Dirt in Oil

Put a slice of raw potato in used oil and watch the dirt settle down at the bottom of the pan. Now it is ready to be reused again.

Spongy Paneer

Paneer will turn out spongy if you add half a cup of cream to one litre milk while making 'Paneer'. OR use sour curd instead of vinegar or lemon juice to curdle the milk

To keep Cheese Fresh

Put a pinch of sugar in the cheese box to keep the cheese fresh and free from fungus.

Save Sugar

Adding a teaspoon of glycerine while making jam will save you 100g sugar.

To long last Masala Powder

Home ground masala powder will last longer, if add a teaspoon of vinegar to it before storing.

Planting Pumpkin seeds

Before planting pumpkin seeds or beans, soak them in water for a day for faster sprouting.

Preserving Mint Leaves

An excellent way to preserve fresh mint leaves and celery is to put a few leaves with water in ice trays and freeze. When ever you need to use them in a curry, drop a couple of cubes in.

Ripen Raw Fruits

Raw fruits will ripen in no time, if you place them in a brown paper bag.

Neutralise excess Salt

Neutralise any salty curry by adding milk, milk cream, pricked boiled potatoes, a pinch of sugar, lightly roasted gram flour or balls made of chapati dough to it.

Keep Ants at bay

Add three to four cloves to the sugar container to keep ants at bay.

For delicious flavour

Powdered dry orange peel, added to 'rasam', gives it a delicious flavour.

Kitchen Tips

Freshness of Ghee

To retain the freshness of Ghee, place a lump of rock salt in the container.

Freshness of Papad

Papads will retain their freshness, if you keep them in a sealed paper or polythene bag.

Burnt Food

Burnt food that is stuck to the bottom of the vessel can be easily removed by pouring boiling water in to it along with some chopped onion. Keep aside for five minutes and then clean.

Leftover Idli batter

Leftover Idli and Dosa batter will not turn sour if you place a beetle leaf on top of the batter.

Soft Paneer

Instead of frying paneer immerse it in boiling water. The paneer will remain soft and not break easily.

Bitterness of Methi leaves

To remove the bitterness of Methi leaves, wash them, add a pinch of salt and turmeric powder and keep aside for three hours. Then wash with cold water.

Soft and Tasty Idlis

To make soft and tasty Idlis and Dosas, soak a teaspoon of fenugreek seeds along with the rice and dal.

Bad odour in refrigerator

To prevent bad odour in the refrigerator, wipe the interiors with a cloth soaked in Vanilla essence.

Coffee Powder Hardens

When Coffee powder hardens in the coffee jar, add lukewarm water, shake well and keep it in the refrigerator. You can use it till the last drop as and when needed.

Cleaning Kitchen

Clean your kitchen platform with water to which a capful of vinegar has been added, to keep it free from ants.

Instant Bhaturas

For instant Bhaturas, knead the dough with soda water instead of plain water.

Saving Oil

While frying Pakoras, put in 10g of tamarind for every one kg of oil, to reduce the absorption of oil.

Burnt cooking pan

To clean a burnt cooking pan, slice an onion and boiling it along with salt and water in the pan. Clean when cool.

Unclog Wash basin

Unclog a sink or wash basin by pouring half a cup of vinegar in the drain pipe. Leave overnight, and then pour two mugs of hot water down the drain. The pipe will clear itself.

Keep Vegetables fresh

To keep green vegetables fresh for a long time in the refrigerator, wrap them in news paper or in a silver foil.

For Crispy Pakoras

To make Pakoras crispy, add two tablespoons of rice flour to the gram flour batter.

Lime Pickle

You can make nice Lime Pickle, if you sprinkle Black Pepper over the lemon rind pieces and dry them in the sun.

Prevent insects

To prevent tiny insects invading you dals, put a little bit of oil on them when storing in the container.

Preserve Tomatoes

To preserve tomatoes, liquidise them, spread the puree on a plastic sheet and dry in the sun.

By evening it will be dry. Crumble and store in n airtight bottle. This dried tomato is free of chemicals and preservatives and remains fresh for months.

For Crispy biscuits

Biscuits will stay crisp, if you put a couple of sugar lumps in the tin.

Cut Apple slices

Apple slices will remain fresh and won't get discolour if kept in salted water.

Left over sweets

Leftover sweets or Burfi make excellent fillings for sweet puris or parathas.

While Peeling Onions

If you chew gum while peeling onions, your eyes will not water. OR

Store onions in the fridge for half an hour before chopping them.

More Juice from Fruits

Citrus fruits such as oranges and lemons will yield more juice if they are heated in the oven for a few minutes before being squeezed.

Prevent Moisture in Salt

To prevent moisture getting in to salt in the rainy season, drop a few rice grains in the salt jar.

Nutritious Salad

To make a tangy, nutritious salad, heat two teaspoons of oil and add a few mustard seeds in to it. Toss in chopped cabbage and stir-fry for few minutes. Cool and serve.

Smell of Corriander leaves

To remove the smell of corriander leaves, garlic or any leafy vegetable from your hands, rub them with toothpaste and wash the odours away.

Sourness of Tomato

To reduce the sourness of tomatoes while cooking a paneer curry, add milk instead of water.

Traces of Pesticides

To remove traces of pesticides, soak fruits and vegetables for a few minutes in a bowl of cold water to which three table spoons of vinegar has been added.

To Prevent Cockroaches

Keep betel nuts in kitchen cabinets to ward off cockroaches.

To keep Almonds fresh

Add one teaspoon of sugar to a container of almonds to keep them fresh longer.

Foul smell from dust bin

To remove the foul smell from the insides of a dustbin, sprinkle some salt at the bottom.

To prevent worms

To get rid of worms from stored rice, sprinkle powdered salt on it.

Peel Orange quickly

Immerse orange in boiling water for five minutes to help you peel them quickly and easily separate the segments.

Remove Burnt Food Stains

To remove burnt food stains from a non-stick pan, heat the pan and saut`e ripe banana pieces in it for some time. The marks will disappear.

Re-use of Silver foils

Remove the foil from an empty carton of tea leaves and use it to store food in the refrigerator, or cover tiles behind the gas stoves in the kitchen.

Preserve natural colour of Fruit

To prevent fresh fruit from becoming brown, place them in lemon juice or grape fruit juice.

Preserve Lemon

When you need only a few drops of Lemon

juice, make a small hole in the lemon and squeeze the desired quantity. Then put the lemon back in the fridge.

Remove excess Oil

To remove excess grease or oil from soups and lentils, stir few ice cubes in it and then take it out. You will find grease will stick to the ice cubes.

Retain natural colour

To retain the original colour of fruits, add a few drops of lemon juice to the fruits after cutting them.

While cooking spinach, add a pinch of baking soda to get pure green colour and add ½ tsp. of sugar to carrots, peas and beans to remain natural colour.

Shine copper utensils

To shine copper utensils, rub lightly with salt and vinegar and wash as usual.

Remove stains from Tea Cups

To remove stains from tea cups, apply a paste of baking soda and salt.

Preserve shine of crystal objects

To bring the shine back from crystal objects, make a mixture of vinegar and lukewarm water, and wash them with this mixture.

Separate glasses

When two glasses adhere to each other, fill the top glass with cold water and place the bottom glass in hot water. Gently pull the top glass away.

Protect glassware from breaking

It is better to wash glassware and china plates by placing the rubber mat on the bottom of the sink. So you can protect them from cracking or chipping.

Keep Ice-cream fresh

To keep the ice-cream fresh for a long time in the freezer, cover the ice cream box first with an aluminium foil.

Sharpen Knife

To sharpen the knife, simply rub on the matchbox (striking strip side).

Remove rust stains from cutlery

To remove the rust stains from the forks and knives, apply onion juice on them, and keep for an hour, then rinse and dry well.

While boiling Eggs

To ensure that eggs do not crack when boiling, add some salt to the water.

Smell of Fish

To get rid of the smell of fish, wash your hand with rice water.

Glossary

A

AJWAIN (AJMA, BISHOP'S WEED, CAROM SEEDS) - In India, it is also called "Bishop's Weed". The fragrance of the spice is very similar to that of cumin.

ALLSPICE [SPICE] - Indian cookery depends wholly on using the right blend of spices. That is why traditional combinations of spices are home-ground and kept ready for use. The term for these mixtures is "masala". Each region of India has its own special blend depending on availability, climate and methods of cooking.

AMCHUR POWDER (DRIED MANGO POWDER) - Mango powder is made from raw, sour, green mangoes

ANISEED (SAUNF) - In India, it is roasted and eaten after meals as a mouth freshener and to stimulate digestion.

B

BRINJAL (BAINGAN, EGGPLANT) - It is an elongated or rounded vegetable with a smooth, shiny, purple skin covering a light firm flesh.

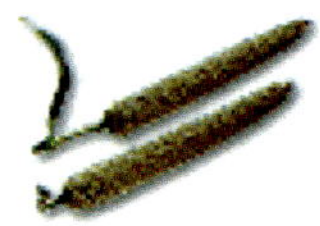

MILLET (BAJRA) - Bajra is a very popular cereal eaten along the Western coastal region of India.

BAKED BEANS - Baked beans is a convenience food available in cans at most grocery stores. It consists of small haricot beans cooked in tomato sauce flavoured with spices and seasonings.

BAKING POWDER - Baking powder is a raising (leavening) agent that is a mixture of sodium bi-carbonate (soda bi-carb), cream of tartar and starch.

BAKING SODA (SODA BI-CARB, SODIUM BI-CARBONATE) - It is a white, alkaline powder which is used in cookery to soften water for cooking vegetables quickly and to preserve the colour of green vegetables.

BASIL (TULSI) [SPICE] - It is a sacred plant for the Hindus, with lots of medicinal properties. The leaves have a sweet smell.

BASMATI RICE - It is a variety of polished Indian rice that has a rich aroma once it is cooked.

BAY LEAVES (TEJ PATTA) - The dry light green coloured long aromatic leaves are preserved in an airtight bottle.

BEAN SPROUTS - "Bean Sprouts" are actually sprouted moong beans and are easy to make at home.

BEETROOT (CHUKANDAR) - It is a very red, rather fat root with leaves like Swiss Chard. Beetroot has a fine dark red flesh.

BLACK CHICKPEAS (KALA CHANA) - Found mainly in coastal and Central India, black chickpeas are also referred to as wild peas.

BLACK EYED BEANS (CHAWLI, CHOLA DAL, LOBHIA) - Produced in pods on small bushy plants, black-eyed beans.

BLACK LENTILS (BLACK GRAM, URAD, URAD DAL, WHOLE URAD DAL) - Black lentils commonly known as urad dal are used in its whole form in North Indian cookery, whereas split black lentils are used in the South.

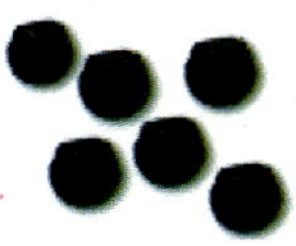

BLACK PEPPERCORNS (KALA MIRCH) - Fresh green peppercorns in bunches are used in pickles.

BLACK SALT (KALA NAMAK OR SANCHAL) - It is a purplish brown coloured rock salt, with a distinctive flavour.

BLACK SESAME SEEDS (KALA TIL) - Chinese sesame seeds are black in colour.

BUTTERMILK (TAAK) - Buttermilk refers to the slightly sour liquid obtained after churning cream.

C

CARAWAY SEEDS (SHAHJEERA, SIYAJEERA) [SPICE] - A native of Europe, Asia & North Africa, they are very small dark brown seeds and look very similar to the normal cumin seeds.

CARDAMOM (ELAICHI) [SPICE] - Cardamom is known as the queen of spices.

CAROM SEEDS (AJWAIN) [SPICE] - Very tiny brown seeds with strong smell.

CASHEWNUTS (KAJU) [SPICE] - Cashewnuts thrive along the coastline of India. The cashew fruit is a fleshy, juicy, sweet, bellshaped fruit.

CELERY (CELERY LEAVES, CELERY STALKS, CELERY STEMS) - A vegetable grown for its roots, stems, leaves and seeds.

CHILLI POWDER (PAPRIKA) [SPICE] - Dried red chillies are powdered finely to get chilli powdered.

CHILLIES (HARI MIRCH, LAL MIRCH, PAPRIKA) [SPICE] - Chillies come in many forms like fresh, dried, powdered or used in making curries, sauces etc.

CHUTNEYS - A sweet, spicy, sour or tangy condiment, chutney is used as an accompaniment or as an ingredient to various savouries.

CINNAMON (DALCHINI) [SPICE] - Cinnamon is the evergreen tree of the Laurel family. The inner bark of the cinnamon tree is the spice that is used in cooking.

CLOVES (LAUNG, LAVANG) [SPICE] - Is a dried aromatic flower bud of a clove tree.

CORIANDER (CILANTROV)

CORN (MAIZE, MAKKAI) - Corn is a cereal which is white, yellow or rust in colour.

CORNFLOUR (CORNMEAL, MAKKAI KA ATTA, MAIZE FLOUR) - Cornflour is obtained by finely milling the dried corn grain. Cornflour is fine, white and soft in appearance. It is odourless and has a mild taste.

COTTAGE CHEESE (PANEER, CHENNA) - Cottage cheese is obtained from milk (either full fat or skimmed milk), coagulated by the action of heat and acid. The resulting whey is drained out to get cottage cheese or paneer. It is knobbly textured, mild flavoured and white in appearance.

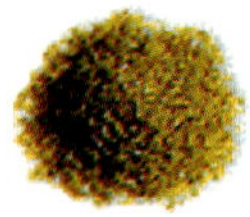

CRACKED WHEAT (BROKEN WHEAT, BULGUR, BURGHUL, DALIA, FADA,LAPSI) - Cracked wheat is also known as Bulgar wheat or broken wheat. It is made by milling wheat grains coarsely.

CUMMIN SEEDS (JEERA) [SPICE] - Cumin is the seed of a small slender herb of the corriander family. These aromatic small seeds which give out more aroma when roasted or added to hot oil. Cummin seeds whole or in powdered form are very commonly used in Indian cooking.

CURDS (DAHI) - Curds are made by coagulating milk with the help of a fermenting agent.

CURRY LEAVES (KADHI PATTA, LIMBDA, MEETHA NEEM) - Aromatic leaves used fresh and generously in many Indian dishes, especially in the South.

CUSTARD APPLE (SITAPHAL) - The fruit is the size of an orange with a rough green skin which turns blackish brown when the fruit is fully ripe.

CUSTARD POWDER - Custard powder is a commercially produced mixture of cornflour, colour and flavour to make custard sauce.

D

DATES (KHAJUR) - Dates are the fruit of the date palm. They are brown and fleshy, about 4 cm. (1 1/2") long and grow in clusters.

DESSICATED COCONUT (SPICE) - These are dry white tiny flakes of coconut.

DRIED FENUGREEK LEAVES (KASOORI METHI)

DRIED MILK (MILK POWDER, POWDERED MILK)

DRIED PEANUTS (GROUND NUTS, PEANUTS, MOOMFALI) - Dark pink, brittle and dry in appearance. They have a pleasant aroma and are bland, floury and can be easily chewed. sauces.

DRIED PEAS (BLACK VATANA, RAGDA, SUKHA MUTTER)

E

EDIBLE SILVER FOIL (VARAK, VARQ) - Edible silver leaf is added as a garnish over sweets. Silver foil is as thin as the best chiffon and lustrous. It is extremely fragile and often breaks up during use. It has no aroma or taste. It is sold between sheets of tissue paper. Edible silver foil is used only as a garnish for sweets, rich biryanis and kebabs.

ESSENCE (FRAGRANCE) - An essence is a concentrated aromatic liquid used either to enhance the flavour of certain culinary preparations or to flavour certain foods that have little or no flavour of their own. Essences have been a part of Indian cookery since antiquity. Even today, they are used at festive functions, in ritual worshop and at traditional weddings. Essence are of two kinds : 1. Plant Extracts or Natural Essences.

F

FENNEL (BADISAUNF) - It is a bigger but milder variety of the aniseed family. In India fennel seeds are used in flavouring many vegetable dishes and pickles. It is roasted and eaten after meals as mouth freshener.

FENUGREEK (KASURI METHI, METHI, METHI BHAJI, METHI LEAVES, METHI SEEDS) [SPICE] - Fenugreek is a perennial herb that grows 30 to 60 cm. tall and is very easy to grow in mild climates. It produces thin oval leaves which are bitter in taste. The leaves are eaten as a vegetable throughout India. The fresh stalks with leaves are sold in every Indian food shop. The leaves are eaten in a number of ways. Fenugreek leaves are rich in iron, vitamins and minerals. They are used in pickles and for flavouring vegetable and curries. Fenugreek seeds are used to flavour all sorts of Indian savouries and some sweets like ladoos. They are an essential ingredient in curry powder and are widely used in South Indian cookery in batters, chutneys and lentils. Fenugreek is one of the most powerful Indian spices that has a bitter and lingering taste.

FIG (ANJEER) - It is the fruit of the fig tree, which is pear-shaped or globular. It is eaten both fresh and dried. Fresh Figs being the sweetest of all fruits, are usually eaten in their natural state. They can also be cooked and used in hot and cold desserts.

Dried Figs Dried figs are made from very ripe figs which are sun-dried. They are flattened in appearance, have a high calorific value and are rich in sugar and vitamins.

FRENCH BEANS (BALKA, FANSI) - Different varieties from pale green or yellow to dark green are available. French beans have a low calorific value and are nutritious. They should be trim crisp with a good green appearance and not very string or hard. They are cooked in boiling water or can be stir fried also.

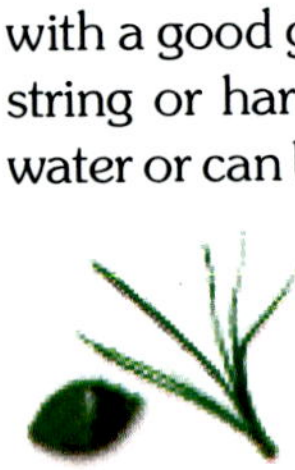

FRESH GREEN GARLIC - It has a fresher, more delicate flavour than garlic cloves. It consists of one small clove at the base of a long slender stem which is green in colour. The cloves are usually tied in bunches and are freely available during the winter months. They are used to flavour vegetable dishes, parathas and also to make a Gujarati dish called "Oondhia".

G

GANTHIA - It is a popular savoury snack made from a batter of spiced gram flour or besan. This is then pressed through special moulds and deep fried until crisp in texture. Different moulds are used for making different shapes of ganthia or vermicelli.

GARAM MASALA (MIXTURE OF SPICES) [SPICE] - Indian cookery depends wholly on using the right blend of spices. That is why traditional combinations of spices are home-ground and kept ready for use. The term for these mixtures is "masala". Each region of India has its own special blend depending on availability, climate and methods of cooking.

GARDEN MINT [SPICE] - Garden mint is the most common variety of mints. Its leaves are used to make chutneys, to flavour sauces and salads and in cooking vegetables.

GARLIC (LAHSUN, GARLIC CLOVES) [SPICE] - It is a strong smelling bulb with segments known as cloves. The aroma of garlic is unmistakable and pungent. The smell has an undernote of sulphur and the taste can be quite sharp and biting. Dried garlic, garlic oil, garlic powder and flakes are the common forms of garlic. It has a lot of medicinal value. It is supposed to purify blood and reduce cholestrol. It enhances the flavour of curries, chutneys and pickles.

GINGER (ADRAK, SOONTH) [SPICE] - Ginger is the underground stem or rhizome of a herbacous plant with long, thin stalks and leaves. The rhizomes are dug up while still tender, if they are to be used fresh. If they are to be dried, they are harvested when it is more fibrous and mature. Fresh ginger is bulbous, tan or pale beige in colour and is firm. It has a cream or yellow interior which is fibrous, but easy to slice. Powdered ginger (Soonth) is used in preparing confectioneries ginger biscuits etc.

GRAM (BENGAL GRAM, CHANA) - Gram or Bengal gram as it is also known, is the most widely grown lentil in India. Whole Bengal Gram are reddish brown in colour, round with a fairly thick skin and conceal a yellow centre. Whole lentils are musky, chewy and coarse.

GRAPES (ANGOOR, DRAKSH, KISHMISH, RAISINS, SULTANAS) - Grapes are fruits of a vine which grows in bunches on a stalk. The skin may be green, yellow or purple and they enclose a sweet but acid pulp with or without seeds. There are also varieties cultivated as dessert grapes, which are served as fresh fruit or used in cooking. Grapes are used in patisserie and other forms of cookery. They are used in tarts and flans, fruit salads and rice dishes.

GUAVA (PERU) - It is apple or pear shaped (depending on its variety) with a thin olive to yellow skin and covers a pink, white or yellow pulp. Highly flavoured, refreshing, yet rather sour, it contains a large number of hard seeds. The fruit is one of the very good sources of Vitamin C. When ripe, it is eaten on its own. It is also used to make drinks, ice-creams and jellies.

H

HONEY (MOHA, MADH, SHAED) - It is a sweet substance manufactured by bees from the nectar obtained by them from flowers which is stored in the cells of the hive as food.

I

ICING SUGAR - It is granulated sugar milled very finely to a powder mixed with 3% starch in France, calcium, phosphate in Britain and cornflour (cornstarch) in the United States, to prevent it from caking.

L

LIME (LIMBOO, LEMON, LIME, NIMBU, SOUR LIME

LEMON GRASS ((HARI CHAI KI PATTI) - Lemon grass is a perennial, aromatic, tall grass with rhizomes and densely tufted fibrous roots. Fragrant lemon grass grows in gardens all over India.

LETTUCE (SALAD KA PATTA,SALAD LEAVES) - It is a plant that grows wild all over the

Northern hemisphere and is cultivated in many varieties for its large edible leaves.

M

MACE (ARIL, JAVINTRI, JAVITRI) - Mace is a lacy scarlet filigree closely enveloping the hard kernel which is nutmeg.

MELON (CANTALOUPE, HONEYDEW MELON, KALINGAD, MUSKMELON, WATERMELON)

MELON SEEDS (CHAR MAGAZ)

MINT (PUDINA)

MOONG BEANS (BEAN SPROUTS, MAG, SPLIT MOONG BEANS, WHOLE MOONG)

MOONG DAL (SKINNED MOONG BEANS, SPLIT MOONG BEANS, YELLOW MOONG DAL) - Whole yellow lentils are split to obtain moong dal.

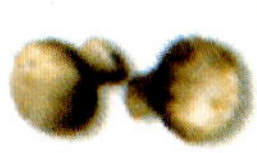

MUSHROOMS (CHAMPIGNON, DHINGRI, GUCCHI, KHUMB, KHUMBH) - Mushrooms are a kind of fungus generally found growing in cool damp places in the woods where there is rich soil.

MUSTARD (RAI, RAI NA KURIA, SARSON, SPLIT MUSTARD SEEDS, SARSON KA TEL)

N

NUTMEG (JAIFAL, JAIPHAL) - Nutmeg comes from an evergreen tree that is usually high with dark leaves and fruits, which look like apricots. When ripe, the fruit bursts open. It contains a hard kernel which is nutmeg.

O

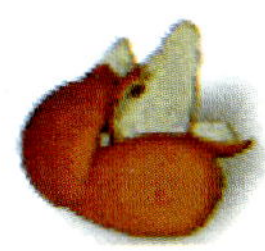

ORANGE RIND (ORANGE PEEL) - The orange zest is obtained by grating or peeling the rind with a zester or a sharp knife as thinly as possible without touching the white inner skin.

P

PAV (BREAD) - Square shaped white bread rolls.

PEACH - A roundish fruit with a fuzzy skin, that is orangish-red in colour. Peaches have a delicate fine textured flesh which is full of flavour.

PEANUTS (GROUNDNUTS, MOONGPHALI, ROASTED PEANUTS, SINGDANA)

PEAR (NASHPATI) - It is the fruit of the pear tree. The fruit is narrow towards the stalk and broadens at the base. The rind is pale green to reddish green in colour and is edible.

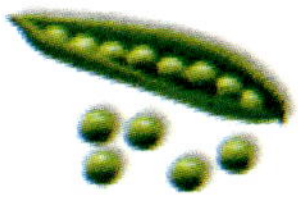

PEAS (FROZEN PEAS, GREEN PEAS, MUTTER, VATANA) - Peas are the small round seeds which are enclosed in a long green pod. Good peas are shiny but not too large and tender.

PISTACHIO NUTS (PISTA) - The pistachio nut is about the size of an olive and the pale green kernel is surrounded by a reddish skin. It is enclosed in a smooth pale reddish brown shell which can easily be split into two.

PLUM (ALU-BOKHARA) - It is a juicy, yet fairly acidic fruit with quite a high sugar content and contains potassium, calcium and vitamins.

POMEGRANATE (ANARDANA, DRIED POMEGRANATE SEEDS, POMEGRANATE SEEDS) - The pomegranate fruit is shiny red to pink in colour and is crowned by a calyx. When opened, angular seeds can be seen inside the translucent red or pink flesh.

PAPADS (APLAM, POPPADUMS) - Papads are round, wafer thin discs made of various lentil or cereal flours.

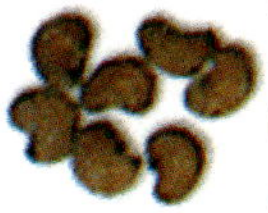

POPPY SEEDS (KHUS-KHUS) - The word poppy instantly brings to mind opium which is obtained from the poppy plant.

POTATO (ALOO, ALU, BATATA)

PUMPKIN (KADDU, LAL BHOPLA) -Pumpkin is round with a flattened top and base. It has an orange or yellow ribbed rind.

R

RADISH (MULA, MULI, PINK RADISH, REDRADISH, WHITE RADISH) - It is a plant of the cabbage family and is cultivated all over the world for its edible root and leaves.

RAISINS (KISHMISH, MANUKA, SULTANANS) - Raisins are dark brown or black in colour and are made from sun-dried black grapes.

RAW MANGO (KACCHA AAM, KAIRI) - Raw mango is the unripe mango.

RED CHILLI POWDER (LAL MIRCH)

RAJMA (RED KIDNEY BEANS) - Large and deep maroon in colour, good red kidney beans are upto 20 mm. (3/4") long.

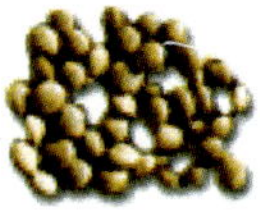

RED LENTILS (MASOOR, MASOOR DAL, SPLIT RED LENTILS) - Red lentils are the seeds of a bushy plant contained in long pods which are plucked, dried and threshed.

REFINED FLOUR (MAIDA, PLAIN FLOUR) - Refined flour is produced by milling the endosperm of the wheat kernel. The wheat kernel is made up of three parts, the endosperm, wheat germ and wheat bran.

RICE SEMOLINA (CHAVAL KA ATTA, GROUND RICE, RICE FLOUR) - It made by milling white rice.

S

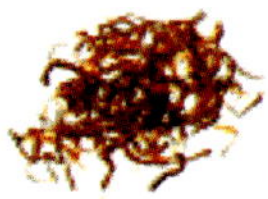

SAFFRON (KESAR, ZAFRAN) - Saffron is the dried stigma of the saffron crocus plant.

SABUDANA (SAGO) - Sabudana is made from the viscous sap of a tall, shady tree. A groove is cut in the trunk of the sabudana palm at intervals and the sap which oozes out is collected. It is then strained through special sieves which form it into little, soft droplets which are dried until hard.

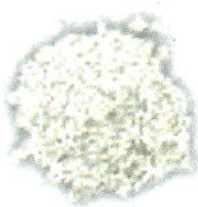

SALT (NAMAK)

SEMOLINA (RAVA, SOOJI) - Semolina is made by processing wheat into tiny grains.

SESAME SEEDS (TIL) - Sesame seeds differ in appearance according to the variety. The most common type used in India is cream coloured, small and glossy.

SOYA SAUCE - It is black in colour and made from soya beans, wheat, water and salt.

SPINACH (PALAK) - It is a vegetable with dark-green curled or smooth leaves.

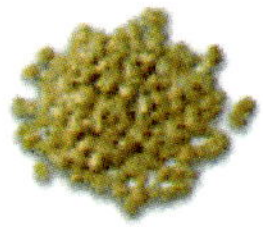

SPLIT BLACK LENTILS (URAD DAL, SKINNED LENTILS)

SPLIT MOONG BEANS (SPLIT GREEM GRAM, SPLIT GREEN MOONG DAL) - They are whole Moong Beans which are split but left in the skin.

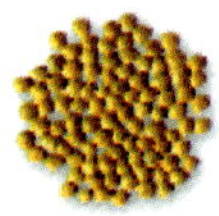

SPLIT RED LENTILS (MASOOR DAL) - Split red lentils are the familiar orange lentils found in grocery shops. Red lentils are delicate in flavour and have a nutty, fresh taste.

SPRING ONIONS (SCALLIONS) - Sold in bunches with their stalks left on, they are either served raw and salted or in salads (the stalks are also used for flavouring).

STRAWBERRY (STRAWBERRY CRUSH, STRAWBERRY PUREE) - Strawberry refers to the red, roughly conical fruit of the strawberry plant.

SUBJA SEEDS (FALOODA SEEDS, TAKHMARIYA) - Subja seeds grow on a variety of basil plants, found all over India. The seeds are tiny, black and tear drop shaped.

SWEET CORN (AMERICAN CORN) - It is another variety of the grain corn. Sweet corn has pale yellow tender milky grains.

SWEET LIME (MOSAMBI) - It is a citrus fruit resembling a lemon in appearance.

SWEET POTATO (SHAKARKAND, SHAKKARIA) - It is an edible tuber which has a reddish, violet or grey skin and a sweet and floury flesh, that is orange-yellow, pink or violet in colour.

T

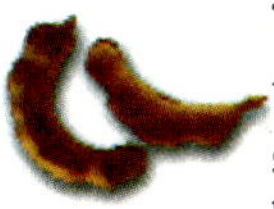

TAMARIND (IMLI) - The tamarind pod is crescent-shaped and brown with a thin brittle shell.

TOMATO (CHERRY TOMATOES, GREEN TOMATOES, TAMATAR, TOMATO JUICE, TOMATO PUREE) - It is a plant cultivated for its red fruits, which are widely used, cooked or raw, in vegetables, in salads, to make sauces, in juices etc.

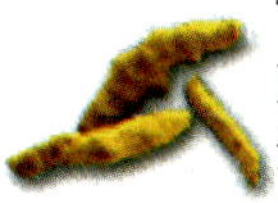

TURMERIC (HALDI) [SPICE] - It is a member of the ginger family. Turmeric, the spice, is the underground root or rhizome of the plant.

V

VERMICELLI (SEVIAN) - Vermicelli is a kind of pasta made from wheat flour.

VINEGAR (BROWN VINEGAR, COOKING VINEGAR, SIRKA) - Vinegar is made by the fermentation of any alcohol. It is clear and transparent and has a sour, acidic aroma and taste.

W

WALNUTS (AKHROT) - Walnuts are the fruit of the walnut tree which grows in Europe and India. French walnuts are well known as are the Kashmiri walnuts.

WATERMELON (KALINGAD, TARBUJ, MELON) - They are large spherical or oval in shape, weighing 3 to 5 kgs. They have a dark green rind and dark pink to reddish flesh that is sweet and very refreshing.

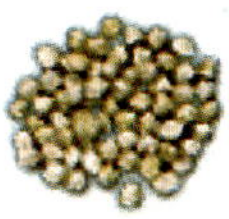

WHITE CHICKPEAS (CHICK PEAS, CHOLE, KABULI CHANNA) - These peas are small, hard, creamy white with a thick skin which often comes away after soaking in water.

WHOLEWHEAT BREAD (CHAPPATI) - It is made from wholewheat flour and yeast.

This is called to as brown bread because it is darker in colour than white bread which is made with refined flour.

Y

YEAST - Yeast is a microscopic fungus that multiplies rapidly in suitable conditions and is used as a raising (leavening) agent in various kinds of dough.

YELLOW LENTILS (ARHAR, TOOVAR DAL)

Z

ZUCCHINI (COURGETTE) - It is variety of marrow (summer squash). It has a shiny green outer skin and a firm, white, watery flesh.